Things To Do In Retirement

101 Budget-Friendly Activities and Pursuits to Help Keep You Healthy & Build Social Connections, Live with Purpose and Enjoy This New Chapter of Your Life!

Kay Atkinson

Contents

Introduction	5
1. Discovering Purpose Post-Retirement	9
2. Staying Connected and Building New Relationships	29
3. Embracing Technology in Retirement	47
4. Health, Fitness, and Well-Being	65
5. Creative Pursuits and Learning	85
6. Outdoor and Nature Activities	105
7. Travel and Exploration	123
8. Managing Your Retirement Fun Budget	141
Conclusion	157
References	161

Introduction

Richard was sat there in his porch in the spring summer air, having a cup of coffee and pondering about life. He had just retired as an accountant after forty years and after decades of routine felt both daunted and liberated at the expanse of free time stretching ahead of him. He needn't have worried as shortly afterwards everything changed. He discovered a local art club which reignited his long forgotten passion for painting. Not only that, he had been introduced to a community of like-minded individuals who had brought new energy and purpose to his days. He felt transformed as if this activity had redefined his identity and he looked forward to more in his retirement.

This book was born out of a desire to help people like Richard, and people like you, navigate the unchartered waters of retirement. My experience over the years in education, coaching and personal development has given me insight into the challenges that retirement brings. It has also shown me what enormous opportunities it brings. I have seen firsthand the transformative impact of engaging in meaningful activities in this chapter of your life and it is these that I would like to share with you. My experience, coupled with extensive research and feedback from retirees themselves has enabled me to craft this guide to help you find activities that not only fill your time, but are pathways to finding purpose, health and joy.

'Things to do in Retirement" is structured into three parts. We begin with 'Laying the Foundation for a Fulfilling Retirement, where we explore what this fulfillment might mean to you personally. A little self-exploration. The second section is 'Exploring Activities and Hobbies' which introduces you to many activities that may interest you, taking into account diverse interests, physical capabilities and finances. The third part is 'Planning for Adventures and Experiences'. This section encourages you to step out of your comfort zone and bring excitement to your life. The journey through the book is from introspection through to action and will turn the contemplation into a joyful retirement.

As you move away from your work life you may be fearful of isolation, of feeling lost in unstructured days or worried that you will be bored. The future may feel uncertain, and this book is there to equip you with practical advice and emotional support to help you need that fulfilled life. Through the engaging narratives, expert opinions, and actionable advice in this guide, I want to make you feel seen, understood and inspired. The stories and suggestions that have come from direct feedback from retirees who have walked this path before you are invaluable in shaping content that resonates and delivers.

Endorsements from leading experts in gerontology and life transitions underscore the value and impact of this guide. As one reader commented "This book didn't just suggest activities; it awakened a zest for life I thought I had lost".

What sets this guide apart is its commitment to inclusivity. It considers the different budgets, physical abilities, and interests of retirees. You may be looking for low key activities close to home or adventures that will take you far afield and this book will offer a balance of inspiration and practical advice.

As you turn each page, you will find interactive worksheets and exercises to complete. These are all designed to personalize your journey. They are to inspire action and reflection as well as planning activities so you can make your retirement journey as enriching as possible.

Welcome to your dream retirement – it is time to make it your own!

1. Discovering Purpose Post-Retirement

As the dawn of retirement unfolds, it is not uncommon to encounter a mix of exhilaration and uncertainty. You've likely anticipated this freedom, yet now you face the question of how to fill your days meaningfully. This chapter is your starting point in sculpting a retirement that resonates deeply with your personal aspirations, health, and joy. Here, we explore how to lay a solid foundation for a purpose-driven retirement, beginning with the creation of a vision board, a powerful tool that serves both as an anchor and a compass.

1.1 Crafting Your Retirement Vision Board

Identify Your Dreams

Begin with gathering images and quotes that inspire you and reflect your aspirations for retirement. This is not just about pasting pictures; it's about envisioning your life in the years to come. Choose images that represent how you want to feel—whether it's peaceful, adventurous, fulfilled, or connected. Do you see yourself exploring ancient ruins in Greece, volunteering at a local animal shelter, or perhaps enjoying peaceful mornings in your garden? Include inspiring quotes that speak to your spirit and motivate you. This collage of dreams serves as a constant reminder of your life's potential and sets the stage for a fulfilling retirement.

When selecting these images and quotes, focus on diversity to encompass various facets of life—travel, relationships, hobbies, and personal growth. This process is deeply personal and should resonate with your unique desires and values. As you sift through magazines, websites, or your own photo collections, be selective and intentional. Each element should contribute to a comprehensive vision that excites and inspires you.

Setting Goals

With your vision board filled with inspiring images and quotes, it's time to distill these inspirations into achievable goals. Setting both short-term and long-term goals allows you to create stepping stones towards your larger aspirations. Short-term goals might include enrolling in a photography class or visiting a nearby national park, while long-term goals could be achieving fluency in a foreign language or completing a significant volunteering project.

Start by writing down specific, measurable, achievable, relevant, and time-bound (SMART) goals next to each image or quote on your vision board. This method ensures your goals are clear and reachable, and it sets a timeline for achieving them. For instance, if you've included an image of the Eiffel Tower, your corresponding goal might be to plan and save for a trip to Paris in the next three years. This structured approach not only organizes your aspirations but also boosts your motivation to turn them into reality.

Visualization as Motivation

Visualization is a potent tool in maintaining motivation. Your vision board isn't just a collection of images; it's a visual representation of what you can achieve. Regularly viewing your board engages your brain's reticular activating system, the part of your brain that helps filter important information and sets the stage for turning your visualizations into reality. Every glance at your board reinforces your goals and strengthens your commitment to them.

Incorporate daily or weekly viewings of your vision board into your routine. Use this time to meditate on your goals, visualize yourself achieving them, and affirm your ability to reach these aspirations. This practice not only keeps your goals at the forefront of your mind but also aligns your daily actions with your larger life vision, providing a continual source of motivation.

Regular Review and Adaptation

Life is dynamic, and your vision for retirement may evolve. That's why revisiting your vision board periodically is crucial. As you achieve goals, discover new interests, or shift your priorities, your board should reflect these changes. This regular review not only keeps your vision board relevant but also gives you a tangible sense of accomplishment as you replace achieved goals with new ones.

Set a schedule for reviewing your vision board—whether it's quarterly, bi-annually, or annually. During these reviews, assess which goals have been achieved, which are in progress, and which may no longer resonate with your aspirations. When I was younger, I did a version of this review every New Year. I would write myself a list of goals for the year ahead. I would put the list in an envelope and then the following New Year as I pondered the new set of goals for the year ahead, I would open the envelope to see what I had achieved. Some goals stayed the same, some had been achieved and some new ones were added.

Your review is not about scrapping unachieved goals but realigning your board to match your current passions and circumstances. This process of adaptation ensures your vision board remains a true reflection of your desires, acting as an ever-evolving roadmap to a fulfilling retirement.

∽

Interactive Element: Vision Board

To aid in the creation of your vision board, here's a simple checklist to ensure you cover all essential aspects:

- Variety of images representing different life areas (travel, hobbies, family, etc.)
- Inspirational quotes that resonate with your values and aspirations
- Space for writing down corresponding SMART goals
- Regular review dates noted on your calendar

This checklist ensures that your vision board is well-rounded, dynamic, and tailored to your evolving retirement dreams, making it an effective tool for motivation and action.

1.2 The Joy of Starting Fresh: New Hobbies for the Newly Retired

Retirement unfolds as a unique opportunity to delve into new hobbies and activities that perhaps were set aside during the demanding years of career and family commitments. The exploration of untapped interests is not merely about filling time; it's a profound journey towards self-discovery and personal fulfillment. To begin this exploration, start by reflecting on past interests or the fleeting hobbies you once enjoyed. Perhaps you collected stamps when you were younger or dabbled in painting during college. Revisiting these past interests can be a stepping stone to discovering new hobbies. Additionally, consider exploring completely new territories. Engage in activities like birdwatching, pottery, or even coding—fields you might never have ventured into before. Attend introductory workshops or classes to get a feel for different hobbies. Local community centers, libraries, and adult education centers often offer a variety of such classes that are both accessible and inviting.

The benefits of cultivating a range of hobbies in retirement are vast and varied. Physically, engaging in new activities can significantly enhance your health, improving everything from motor skills to cardiovascular health, depending on the activity. Mentally, the challenge of learning a new skill can keep your brain active and agile, reducing the risk of cognitive decline. Socially, hobbies often provide opportunities to meet new people and build friendships, combating the common post-retirement risk of social isolation. For instance, joining a hiking club or a knitting group can connect you with a community of people who share similar interests, providing both companionship and a sense of belonging.

Consider the story of Linda, a retired school teacher, who discovered her passion for photography later in life. Initially, Linda took up photography to fill her time and to document her travels. However, as she immersed herself in learning the technical skills and artistic aspects of photography, she found a new way of seeing the world. Photography not only became a hobby for her but a passionate pursuit that brought new friends into her life and took her to places she had never imagined visiting. Her involvement in local photography exhibitions and online communities further enriched her experience, turning what started as a simple hobby into a significant part of her identity in retirement.

For those just starting out with new hobbies, the key is to begin modestly. It's easy to feel overwhelmed if you commit to too much too quickly. Instead, integrate new activities gradually into your routine. If you're interested in gardening, start with a small container garden before committing to a large backyard plot. If you're intrigued by cooking, begin by mastering one new recipe each week. This approach allows you to savor each new learning experience without the pressure to immediately excel or make large investments. It also makes the process of adopting new hobbies manageable and enjoyable, rather than another item on a to-do list. Additionally, remember to celebrate small victories along the way—a successfully baked cake, a new chord learned on the guitar, or simply the joy of a morning spent bird-watching. These accomplishments provide motivation and enrich your retirement days with small, yet significant, achievements and pleasures.

Interactive Element: Hobbies and Interests

Begin with a simple list. Think back to everything you have ever shown an interest in, from when you were a child up to adulthood. Include anything that you are interested in, even if you have never tried them.

Next, research. Using the internet, local message boards and personal contacts, for each one, find out if there are local groups to reflect these interests.

1.3 From Career to Passion Projects: Transitioning Your Skills

The transition from a structured career to a fulfilling retirement can be both exhilarating and daunting. Throughout your career, you've honed a suite of skills and gained invaluable experiences that don't have to become redundant once you retire. Instead, these can be the foundation for meaningful passion projects that not only keep you engaged but also add significant value to your life and the community around you. This transition is not about replacing your former career but rather about transforming your skills into projects that ignite your passion.

Skill Assessment

Begin by conducting a thorough assessment of the skills you have cultivated over your career. This includes not only your professional capabilities but also the soft skills such as leadership, communication, problem-solving, and teamwork. For instance, a retired teacher might find that their skills in educating and mentoring can translate beautifully into creating educational workshops or writing books for young adults. Similarly, someone from a corporate background might discover that their project management or strategic planning skills could be pivotal in organizing community initiatives or starting a small business.

To effectively identify these skills, list all your previous job roles and the responsibilities you handled in each. Reflect on the tasks you found most rewarding or where you excelled the most. It's also insightful to ask colleagues, friends, or family about the skills they see as your strengths, as sometimes an external perspective can highlight abilities you might have overlooked. Once you have a comprehensive list, categorize these skills into groups such as creativity, interaction, leadership, and technical prowess. This categorization helps in pinpointing which areas you might want to focus on in your retirement.

Finding Your Passion Project

With a clear understanding of your skills, the next step is to align these with your interests to identify potential passion projects. This alignment is crucial as it ensures your project is not only a showcase of your capabilities but also a source of joy and fulfillment. Start by listing activities or causes you are passionate about. Perhaps you have always wanted to advocate for environmental conservation, delve into the arts, or help underprivileged communities.

Consider how your skills can serve these interests. For example, someone with a background in marketing and a passion for animal welfare could start a campaign to raise awareness and funds for local animal shelters. Alternatively, if you are skilled in crafts, you could create custom artwork to sell and raise money for charity. The key here is to think creatively about how your skills can intersect with your passions to create impactful projects.

Planning for Success

Any successful project requires careful planning, and passion projects are no exception. Start by setting clear, achievable goals for your project, considering what you hope to accomplish and the impact you wish to have. Break these goals down into actionable steps and set timelines for each. This structured approach not only keeps the project manageable but also provides a clear path towards achieving your objectives.

Resource allocation is another critical aspect of planning. Assess what resources you'll need, including time, money, and possibly volunteers. Create a budget and a schedule that outlines how much time each day or week you'll dedicate to your project. Remember, the beauty of retirement is the flexibility it offers, so it's important to balance your project with other retirement activities and personal downtime.

Community Engagement

Finally, sharing your passion project with the community not only broadens its impact but also opens avenues for collaboration and feedback. Engage local community centers, online forums, or social media groups related to your project's focus to share your work and gather support. This engagement can be tremendously rewarding and enriching, providing both social interaction and constructive feedback.

For instance, if your project involves creating public art installations, involve the community in the design or selection process. This inclusion not only garners greater interest and investment in the project but also ensures it meets the community's needs and preferences. Additionally, consider how you can use your project to mentor others. Sharing your skills and experiences can be incredibly fulfilling and can help others learn and grow, further amplifying the impact of your work.

In summary, transforming your career skills into passion projects during retirement is an excellent way to maintain a sense of purpose, contribute to the community, and keep mentally and socially active. By assessing your skills, aligning them with your passions, planning effectively, and engaging with the community, you can ensure your retirement is not just a time of leisure but also a time of enriching and meaningful contributions.

Interactive element:

Skill assessment List. Make your own list first then ask others who know you to add to it.

Identify from those possible passion projects. For each one of these, take a whole page and think about how this relates to causes and activities that excite you and what possible passion projects there may be. Build on this by investigating groups and contacts who would be useful to contact.

1.4 Volunteer Work That Makes a Difference and Fulfills You

Engaging in volunteer work during retirement is not just a noble endeavor; it is a profound avenue for personal growth, community connection, and the pursuit of passions that align with your deepest values. Choosing the right cause to dedicate your time and energy to can significantly enhance your sense of fulfillment and impact. When selecting a cause, start by reflecting on what issues stir your heart and motivate you to take action. Whether it's environmental conservation, education, animal welfare, or healthcare, the key is to connect with a cause that resonates with your personal beliefs and passions. Consider the issues you always wished you had more time to explore and support during your working years, or think about what global or community challenges evoke a strong desire in you to contribute towards change.

Explore various non-profit organizations, community groups, or online platforms that align with your interests. Attend community meetings or events hosted by these organizations to get a firsthand look at their operations and initiatives. Engaging with the people involved can provide deeper insights into the organization's impact and needs, helping you make a well-informed decision. Moreover, many organizations are in need of specific skills, from accounting to marketing or event planning. Your professional skills can profoundly impact these causes, adding another layer of satisfaction in knowing that your career skills continue to benefit others.

The rewards of giving back through volunteer work are multifaceted. On an emotional level, volunteering has been shown to enhance the volunteer's mood and overall psychological well-being. Regular engagement in volunteer activities can significantly reduce stress, combat depression, and provide a profound sense of purpose. Socially, volunteering offers an opportunity to strengthen old friendships and build new ones. Volunteer groups often bring together a diverse range of individuals, and the shared experiences can create lasting bonds. Moreover, the sense of community and belonging that comes from working with others towards a common goal is incomparable. The social interaction involved in volunteer work is particularly beneficial during retirement, a period that can sometimes lead to feelings of isolation or loneliness.

Finding opportunities for volunteering can be approached through several avenues. Start locally by connecting with community centers, local chapters of national organizations, or faith-based groups. These entities often have information on a variety of volunteer opportunities that cater to different interests and abilities. Another effective method is to use digital platforms dedicated to matching volunteers with organizations in need of help. Websites such as VolunteerMatch, Idealist, or local nonprofit networks can be invaluable resources. These platforms allow you to search for opportunities based on your location, interests, and the skills you wish to offer. For those who prefer or require the flexibility to volunteer from home, many organizations offer remote volunteering opportunities, from virtual tutoring to assisting with digital marketing efforts.

Balancing your commitment to volunteer work with other retirement activities and personal obligations is crucial to ensure that your volunteering remains a source of joy and not a burden. Consider your daily and weekly schedules, and determine how much time you feel comfortable dedicating to volunteer efforts. It may be helpful to start with a small commitment and adjust as you find your rhythm and assess your capacity to manage multiple activities. Communicate openly with the volunteer coordinator about your availability and any adjustments that may need to be made as you balance other aspects of your life. This approach ensures that you can enjoy the richness of volunteering without it overshadowing other important elements of your retirement life.

In essence, volunteering offers a unique blend of personal fulfillment and community service. It allows you to invest your time, skills, and passion in causes that matter deeply to you, all while enhancing your emotional and social well-being. Whether you choose to engage locally or through virtual platforms, the impact of your work can be profound, both for yourself and for the community you serve. As you integrate volunteer work into your retirement, the joy of giving back not only enriches your life but also fortifies the community with your invaluable contributions.

Interactive Element

Find out about local volunteering organisations in your area, or further afield if you prefer.

What areas of life would you like to volunteer in?

1.5 Mentoring the Next Generation: Sharing Your Lifetime of Knowledge

The value of your experiences accumulated over a lifetime is immeasurable, and mentoring offers a profound way to share this wealth of knowledge with others. Throughout your career and personal life, you've navigated challenges, celebrated successes, and learned lessons that are invaluable to those just starting their journeys. By stepping into a mentoring role, you not only have the opportunity to guide others but also to reflect on your own life's journey, seeing the impact of your experiences with fresh eyes. Mentoring can be particularly rewarding in retirement, as it allows you to stay intellectually engaged and connected with others, all while giving back in a meaningful way.

Finding the right mentoring opportunities might seem daunting at first, but many communities and industries are in dire need of experienced individuals willing to share their knowledge. Start by identifying your areas of expertise and interests. Whether your background is in education, engineering, arts, business, or any other field, there are likely individuals out there who can benefit from your insight. Contact local schools, universities, and community centers to inquire about formal mentoring programs that need volunteers. Many educational institutions value the involvement of retirees who bring not only expertise but also patience and wisdom to their interactions with students.

Furthermore, the digital world offers expansive opportunities for mentoring without geographical boundaries. Platforms like Score.org, which focuses on helping small business owners, or MentorCruise.com, which connects tech professionals with learners, can be perfect for those who prefer to mentor from the comfort of their home. These platforms allow you to create a profile detailing your expertise and availability, making it easier to connect with mentees who can truly benefit from your guidance.

When it comes to building meaningful relationships with mentees, it's crucial to establish trust and respect from the outset. Effective mentoring goes beyond merely imparting knowledge; it involves listening actively, empathizing with the mentee's challenges, and providing guidance that encourages growth and self-discovery. Be open about your own experiences, including the failures and how you overcame them. This openness not only humanizes you but also provides your mentees with a realistic perspective on what it takes to overcome obstacles and succeed. Regular meetings, whether in person or online, help in building a rapport and provide a structured way to monitor progress and give feedback. Always aim to be the mentor you once wished you had—someone who not only instructs but also inspires and motivates.

Consider the broader impact of mentoring on both your legacy and the lives of your mentees. Each piece of advice you give, each strategy session you hold, and every encouragement you offer can play a significant part in shaping your mentee's career and personal development. This influence, in turn, extends beyond the individual to benefit their broader community and future generations. Mentoring thus becomes a powerful channel for leaving a lasting impact, creating a ripple effect that perpetuates the cycle of learning and growth. Think of your mentoring relationship as an investment into the future, one where your knowledge and skills continue to contribute long after your direct involvement ends.

By engaging in mentoring, you not only enrich the lives of others but also enhance your own retirement experience. It keeps you connected to evolving fields and new generations, providing fresh perspectives and continual learning opportunities. This engagement is a testament to the enduring value of your professional and personal experiences, positioning you as a key contributor to future successes. As you share your knowledge, you'll find that mentoring is not just about teaching—it's also about learning, growing, and connecting in ways that enrich both your life and those of your mentees.

1.6 Writing Your Memoir: Sharing Your Story with the World

Embarking on the journey of writing your memoir is not just about recounting the past; it's an exploration into the very essence of what has shaped you. This process allows you to preserve cherished memories and share significant life lessons with both current and future generations. To begin, selecting a central theme is crucial. Your memoir should not aim to cover every minor event of your life but rather focus on a theme or series of interconnected events that hold particular significance. This could be centered around a defining period—such as your career, family life, or a particular challenge or success—or it could revolve around the values and insights you've gained over the years.

Once your theme is clear, create an outline to organize your stories into a coherent narrative. Start with major life milestones and fill in with smaller, related anecdotes and reflections that support your theme. This outline will not only guide your writing process but also ensure that your memoir remains focused and engaging. Consider using chronological order for clarity, or perhaps a thematic structure if it better suits your story's message.

As you delve into the writing process, it's imperative to embrace your unique voice. Authenticity should be the cornerstone of your memoir. Your readers—whether they be family members, friends, or a broader audience—are looking to connect with your personal experiences and insights, not a stylized version of your life. Write as if you are having a conversation with a trusted friend. This approach will not only make the writing process more enjoyable for you but also more engaging for your readers.

Preserving personal and family history through your memoir serves a dual purpose. Firstly, it acts as a record of familial events and characteristics, offering future generations a window into their heritage. Secondly, it allows you to reflect on your life's journey, understanding how your experiences have shaped you and sharing the wisdom gained. This preservation is particularly poignant in an era where oral histories are fading, replaced by digital snippets that often lack depth and continuity. It may be the case you want to delve further and find out what your ancestors were up to by researching your family tree.

When it comes to sharing your memoir, there are several publishing options available depending on your goals and resources. Self-publishing is a popular choice for many retirees, as it offers control over every aspect of the publishing process—from the cover design to the marketing and distribution. Platforms like Amazon's Kindle Direct Publishing allow you to reach a global audience with minimal upfront costs. For those looking for a more traditional route, securing a literary agent and pursuing publication through established publishing houses is another viable option, though it can be more challenging and time-consuming.

Alternatively, if your aim is to share your story more informally or you wish to reach a specific audience like family and friends, consider blogging. Starting a blog can be a less daunting way to share your life stories. It allows you to post at your own pace and can also serve as an interactive platform where readers can engage directly with you through comments and discussions. This method not only allows for immediate feedback but also fosters a sense of community around your writing.

For those who may feel overwhelmed by the prospect of writing a full memoir or managing a blog, creating a digital photo book with captions or short stories can be an effective alternative. This method combines visual elements with textual narratives, providing a balance that can be both easier to manage and highly engaging for the audience. Many online platforms provide user-friendly templates and tools for creating beautifully designed photo books that can be printed and bound.

In each of these endeavors, the key is to start with a clear plan, proceed at a pace that feels comfortable to you, and choose a sharing method that aligns with your intentions for the memoir. Whether your goal is to leave a legacy, connect with loved ones, or simply reflect on your life's journey, writing your memoir is a rewarding endeavor that not only preserves your past but also enriches your present. As you share your stories, you reaffirm your experiences and offer others a unique perspective on the world—a truly invaluable gift.

Interactive Element: Your Memoirs

Where to start? Some suggestions.

Write a timeline of your life. Fill in key events. Identify different periods in your life. Add funny stories in these eras. Look at past photos. What do they show?

28   Things To Do In Retirement

Adrian and his brother Tim had led separate lives since they left home, Adrian to University and Tim into industry. Over the years, they saw each other seldom at family weddings or funerals. In retirement, they started emailing each other on a regular basis. Starting with lighthearted chats about family and friends, they then moved to hand written letters and over time their relationship deepened and they began to share more of themselves. Both Adrian and Tim found the opportunity to revisit their childhood and talk about life from a shared perspective, enormously beneficial in both reestablishing a close relationship and making sense of their own origins.

In retirement Adrain got a dog, Bootsie Collins. Daily walks and companionship supplied by Bootsie have enabled Adrian to build exercise into the day and provide structure. Adrian worked as a teacher for many years and continues to mark exam papers once a year, connecting him to his previous work life and his passion of history. Recently he joined a men's group that meets every week which is introducing him to new people and also he has found a meet up with fellow history and walking enthusiasts.

Adrian's love of music and thrift stores have been combined to form a side hustle where he spends many happy hours finding CDs that are now unloved by their old owners and he connects them to people who rejoice in finding an old favourite through eBay. It has brought him to revisit music he has enjoyed throughout his life.

2. Staying Connected and Building New Relationships

Moving away from the workplace, certain social connections may be lost but you are stepping into a new vibrant phase of your life in which you can build new threads of connections, based on shared experiences. You will cultivate new relationships which will bring new happiness into your life. Imagine yourself discovering a book club where each new page you read brings new depth to your thoughts and brings new ideas to explore. Each new activity can bring the seeds of a new friendship to blossom. Such social connections not only enhance your social life but will bolster your mental and emotional well-being.

2.1 Joining Clubs and Groups That Match Your Interests

Exploring Local and Online Groups

The quest for engaging social interactions leads many retirees to explore clubs and groups that resonate with their interests. Whether your passion lies in literature, hiking, or art, there's a community waiting for you. Locally, community centers, libraries, and even local cafes often host groups that welcome new members with open arms. Engage in these settings where common interests pave the way for conversation and connection.

Simultaneously, the digital age offers unprecedented access to communities beyond geographical boundaries. Online platforms like Meetup or specialized forums provide gateways to global groups ranging from philosophy discussions to virtual painting classes. These platforms allow you to maintain an active social life from the comfort of your home, making it especially valuable for those who may face mobility challenges or live in remote areas. The key is to start with a clear idea of what you're passionate about and use both local resources and digital tools to find groups that align with your interests.

Helen's life had always revolved around work with even her social life connected to those she worked with. She often had to entertain clients and having retired she missed the social connection of those lunches. Through a chance conversation with an ex-client, she discovered she too had retired and missed the social connection. They decided to go out for dinner each month and try a new restaurant. Over the next few months others were introduced into this event and soon Helen looked forward to trying a new restaurant each month but more importantly she looked forward to an evening in the company of this fantastic group of people, brought together by chance.

Benefits of Community Involvement

Joining these groups are not just about socializing, they will enable you to weave a support network which builds up your emotional resilience as well as helping keep you mentally healthy. A common feeling in retirement can be loneliness or isolation and this can be alleviated by engaging regularly with these groups. There are studies that suggest that active social activity brings other benefits too; improvement in cognitive function and a contribution towards a longer, healthier life. The stimulation that comes from engaging discussions or collaborative projects in club settings is a potent tonic for the mind and spirit, keeping you engaged and mentally sharp.

Making the First Move

However, taking the first step to join a new group can often be daunting. The apprehension about how you will be received or whether you will find genuine connections can deter even the most sociable individuals. It is essential to approach this with a strategy: start small. You might first attend as a guest or observer, which can provide a sense of the group's dynamics without the pressure to fully commit. Contact the group facilitator ahead of time, expressing your interest and any apprehensions you might have. More often than not, group leaders are eager to assist newcomers in feeling welcome. Remember, every member of the group has been in your shoes at one point and understands the courage it takes to make that first step.

Diverse Interests for Diverse Connections

Embracing a variety of groups can enrich your social experience, exposing you to a broader spectrum of perspectives and activities. While it's comforting to engage with groups where you share common ground, stepping into a club that might be out of your usual comfort zone can be surprisingly rewarding. Perhaps consider joining a technology club to learn new skills, or a storytelling group where you can share and listen to life experiences different from your own. Each group offers unique opportunities to grow and learn, ensuring your retirement is anything but monotonous. It may be that you attend a group and after a few sessions, you are not feeling attached or connected to others within it. It may be the level is too high or too low. Don't be afraid to put it down to experience and try another group!

Case Study: Embracing New Connections

Consider the story of Maria, who relocated to a new city post-retirement and initially felt isolated. Her love for quilting led her to join a local crafting club. Not only did she find camaraderie and support, but she also discovered her knack for teaching others, which added a newfound sense of purpose to her life. Maria's experience underscores the transformative power of taking that first step to engage with a new group.

By actively seeking and participating in various clubs and groups, you not only enrich your retirement life but also lay a foundation for long-lasting relationships that provide support, laughter, and an expanded view of the world around you. As you continue to explore and engage with new communities, each interaction weaves another vibrant thread into the rich tapestry of your retired life, filled with friends, learning, and unforgettable experiences.

2.2 Navigating Social Media to Reconnect and Meet New Friends

In the digital age, social media stands out as a vibrant arena for retirees aiming to reconnect with old friends and forge new friendships. Understanding how to effectively navigate these platforms can significantly enhance your social interactions and expand your circle. To begin, selecting the right social media platforms is crucial. Facebook, with its widespread usage across various age groups, is excellent for reconnecting with people from your past, such as former classmates or co-workers. Its user-friendly interface and features like groups and community pages make it not only accessible but also a rich resource for meeting new people who share your interests.

On the other hand, platforms like Instagram or Pinterest might appeal to those who are more visually inclined and enjoy photography or arts and crafts. These platforms allow you to follow hashtags or join boards that resonate with your hobbies, thus connecting you with individuals who appreciate similar aesthetic pursuits. For those interested in professional networking or keeping in touch with former colleagues, LinkedIn offers a more formal setting to discuss industry trends, share professional advice, and reconnect with peers in a business-oriented environment.

Once you have chosen platforms that align with your interests and comfort level, the next important step is ensuring your online interactions are secure and private. Start by familiarizing yourself with the privacy settings of each platform. Adjust these settings to control who can view your posts, comment on your pictures, or share your content. Be cautious about the personal information you share online; details such as your home address, phone number, or daily routines should be guarded to prevent any potential security risks. Additionally, regularly updating your passwords and using different passwords for different sites can significantly enhance your online safety.

Engaging actively in online communities is another enriching way to utilize social media. Most platforms offer a myriad of groups and forums that bring together people with shared interests. Whether you are a gardening enthusiast, a book lover, or a travel aficionado, there is likely a group that matches your passion. Participating in these groups can be as simple as commenting on a post, sharing your own experiences, or even asking questions. These interactions, while virtual, can lead to meaningful connections and even offline friendships. It's also a platform for you to share your wealth of knowledge and experiences, which can be incredibly fulfilling and appreciated by younger members of the community.

Understanding the etiquette of online interactions is key to maintaining positive and respectful engagements. Each social media platform has its own unspoken rules and norms, but some general principles apply universally. Always communicate online as you would in person—respectfully and thoughtfully. Avoid engaging in or instigating conflicts; if you encounter offensive or inappropriate content, it's wise to use the platform's reporting tools rather than confronting the individual publicly. Show appreciation for others' content by liking, commenting, and sharing posts that you find meaningful. This not only fosters positivity but also encourages a reciprocal appreciation of your posts.

As you explore the diverse landscapes of social media, remember that these tools are not just about consuming content but about creating and participating in a community. Each comment you leave, each post you share, and each connection you make contributes to a larger conversation. With the right approach, social media can be a wonderful resource for maintaining existing relationships and developing new ones, ensuring your social life remains as vibrant and fulfilling as ever.

2.3 Hosting Themed Gatherings for Fellow Retirees

In the vibrant tapestry of retirement, themed gatherings stand out as colorful patches, bringing joy, laughter, and connection. These events are more than just social activities; they are opportunities to foster a sense of community and share experiences that resonate deeply with your peers. When planning such gatherings, the key lies in meticulous preparation and a touch of creativity. Start by considering the interests and commonalities that define your social circle. This might include shared historical eras, mutual hobbies, or even favorite genres of music or literature. Each gathering should aim to reflect these shared threads, creating an atmosphere that feels both unique and personal.

The process of planning your themed gathering should begin with selecting a theme that is not only entertaining but also accessible to all attendees. This consideration is crucial in ensuring that everyone feels welcome and able to participate. For instance, a 'Roaring 20s' jazz night can offer both lively music and a nostalgic touch that many retirees might appreciate. Alternatively, a 'Gardener's Get-together' can be a hit among those who cherish their time in the garden, featuring floral decorations and seed exchange activities. Other theme ideas could include a literary dinner party where each dish is inspired by a famous novel or a classic movie screening night where guests come dressed as their favorite film characters.

Once your theme is set, dive into the logistics of your event. Venue selection is paramount; it should accommodate the needs of all guests, considering factors such as accessibility for those with mobility issues and proximity for those who might not have access to easy transportation. If your home is not suitable, local community centers, outdoor parks, or even rented halls can provide excellent alternatives. Next, consider the decorations, music, and food, all of which should align with your chosen theme to create a cohesive and immersive experience. For instance, if you decide on a '70s disco party, think about installing a temporary dance floor, disco balls, and playing classic hits from that decade to set the right mood.

Building a tight-knit community among peers through regular themed gatherings can transform casual acquaintances into a supportive network of friends. By organizing these events regularly, you encourage ongoing engagement and provide something for your group to look forward to. It's about creating a tradition that everyone values. This regularity not only strengthens bonds but also provides a safe and joyful space for everyone to express themselves and share their stories, which is especially important in combating the feelings of isolation that can sometimes accompany retirement.

Inclusivity should be at the heart of every gathering. This means planning events that cater to a wide range of interests, physical abilities, and dietary needs. Always send out invitations well in advance and ask for RSVPs along with any special requirements your guests might have. This could include dietary restrictions, accessibility needs, or even preferred music if you're planning a dance event. If you are expecting a diverse group, consider having quiet areas for those who might get overwhelmed by loud music or crowds, and ensure that all areas are wheelchair accessible if needed. Activities should also allow everyone to participate, regardless of physical ability. For example, a quiz night or a group storytelling session can be enjoyable and engaging for all attendees without requiring physical exertion.

By meticulously planning your themed gatherings with a focus on creativity, inclusivity, and community building, you create memorable experiences that enrich the lives of all attendees. These events become highlights in the calendars of your peers, eagerly anticipated and fondly remembered, continuing to weave those vibrant threads of connection through the community you cherish.

2.4 Finding and Joining Local Community Events

Immersing yourself in the vibrant tapestry of local community events can open doors to new experiences and connections that enrich your retirement life in unexpected ways. The key to discovering these opportunities lies in knowing where to look and having the willingness to step into new experiences that might be outside your usual routine. Local events ranging from art exhibitions, musical concerts, to farmers' markets and charity runs offer diverse experiences that can enhance your social network and provide substantial engagement with your community.

To begin uncovering these events, start with resources that are readily available and often underutilized. Community boards, both physical and online, are treasure troves of information. Local libraries and community centers typically have bulletin boards filled with flyers and announcements about upcoming events. Similarly, many communities have websites or social media pages dedicated to local happenings where you can subscribe to receive regular updates. Additionally, local newspapers, both in print and online, often have community calendars that list upcoming events. By regularly checking these resources, you can stay informed about what's happening around you and choose which events spark your interest.

Another excellent resource is your local government's website. Many cities and town councils host events such as public town hall meetings, cultural festivals, and seasonal celebrations that not only aim to entertain but also to foster community spirit and engagement. These events are not only opportunities to have fun but also to meet people from different walks of life who share a common interest in bettering the neighborhood and engaging actively in local culture.

While familiarity provides comfort, stepping out of your comfort zone and attending events that you wouldn't normally consider can broaden your horizons significantly. This could mean attending a lecture on modern art, even if you've never set foot in an art gallery, or going to a jazz concert even if you've never listened to jazz before. Each new experience adds layers to your understanding and appreciation of different cultures and communities. It's also an opportunity to meet people with different perspectives and life experiences, which can be both refreshing and enlightening. The key is to approach each event with an open mind and the willingness to engage, allowing yourself to be surprised by how much you enjoy something new.

Volunteering at local events offers another dimension of involvement that can be incredibly rewarding. Many events rely on volunteers to run smoothly, and offering your time can be a great way to give back to the community while engaging with it. Volunteering is not only a noble endeavor but also a powerful way to meet others who share your values of service and community support. Whether it's helping to set up for a local festival, manning a booth at a charity run, or assisting in organizing a community clean-up, each act of volunteering places you at the heart of the community. The dual benefits of personal fulfillment and social engagement make volunteering at local events a fruitful pursuit.

Taking the initiative to organize your own community event or meetup can lead to even deeper connections and satisfactions. This could be as simple as starting a book club, hosting a coffee morning for fellow retirees, or organizing a neighborhood potluck. What starts as a small gathering can grow into a recurring event that others look forward to. The process of organizing these events also sharpens your leadership and planning skills and gives you a direct hand in creating the type of community you want to live in. Start by identifying a need or interest in your community that isn't being met, and then reach out to local venues to see if they would be interested in hosting. Local businesses, especially cafes and bookstores, are often open to hosting community events as it also benefits them. Promote your event through local channels and social media to gather interest and encourage a diverse group of people to attend. By taking the lead in bringing people together, you not only enrich your own social life but also strengthen the fabric of your community.

As you explore, join, and perhaps even lead local community events, remember that each step you take builds a broader, more vibrant social life. These activities allow you to remain an active, engaged, and valued member of your community, continuously learning, sharing, and growing. Whether it's through discovering new interests, stepping into unfamiliar experiences, volunteering, or leading initiatives, your active participation in community events can transform your retirement into a dynamic and fulfilling phase of life, filled with meaningful connections and enriching experiences.

2.5 Traveling in Groups: Adventures with Peers

The allure of exploring new destinations is universally compelling, but when shared with others, the experience can transform from delightful to unforgettable. Group travel, especially among peers who share a stage in life or similar interests, offers a unique blend of camaraderie, excitement, and support. For retirees, the benefits of group travel are particularly attractive, encompassing everything from logistical ease to creating deeper connections through shared experiences.

One of the most significant advantages of traveling in groups is the cost-effectiveness it offers. When you travel with others, many expenses can be shared, reducing the individual cost significantly. Accommodations, transportation like car rentals, and even tour group fees often offer discounts for larger numbers, making that dream trip more financially accessible. More than just savings, group travel alleviates much of the stress associated with planning and navigating unfamiliar places. With shared responsibilities, each member can contribute their strengths, whether in organization, language skills, or knowledge about the destination, making the journey smoother and more enjoyable for everyone involved.

The social aspect of group travel can not be overstated. Exploring new cities, indulging in exotic cuisines, and experiencing unique cultures with peers strengthens bonds and often leads to lasting friendships. These shared experiences provide a collective memory bank that enriches your social interactions long after the trip has ended. For retirees, these connections are invaluable, providing a sense of belonging and community that enhances quality of life. Moreover, traveling in groups offers a sense of safety and security that can encourage more adventurous travel choices, knowing that you have reliable companions who share in the experience and its challenges.

Finding the right travel group is crucial to ensuring the experience is as rewarding as possible. For retirees, many travel agencies and community groups offer specialized travel clubs that cater to older adults. These groups often plan itineraries with the needs of retirees in mind, considering factors like pace, physical demand, and accessibility. Joining established groups can also alleviate the pressure of planning and allow you to focus purely on the enjoyment of the journey. However, if you prefer a more personalized experience, organizing a private travel group with friends can be equally fulfilling. Start by discussing potential destinations with your peers, considering everyone's interests and bucket list items to ensure the itinerary appeals to all involved.

Planning the itinerary for group travel requires thoughtful consideration to ensure it caters to the interests and needs of all group members. Begin by holding a planning meeting to discuss everyone's expectations and any must-visit sites or activities. This initial conversation can help set the tone for the trip and ensure that all members feel heard and excited about the planned activities. When crafting the itinerary, balance is key. Include a mix of structured group activities and free time, allowing for personal exploration or rest, which can be crucial for managing energy levels, especially in groups with varying mobility levels. Consider also the pacing of the trip—plan enough time at each location to avoid the trip feeling rushed but maintain enough movement to keep the itinerary exciting.

Shared travel experiences form some of the most vivid memories, as they encapsulate not only the sights and sounds of new locales but also the laughter, conversations, and camaraderie that come with exploring the world with others. Each shared meal, guided tour, and spontaneous adventure becomes a thread in the fabric of your relationships, woven tightly with joy and mutual experience. These memories are treasures, recalled at group reunions or through photos and stories, continuously strengthening the bonds formed on the road. For retirees, these experiences are not just about seeing new places but about enriching life with meaningful relationships and joyful encounters, making every trip a chapter in a richer, more colorful life narrative.

Traveling with peers offers a unique opportunity to explore, learn, and bond in ways that solo journeys might not provide. As you look forward to your next group adventure, consider not just the destinations but the companions you choose to journey with, for they are the ones who will turn your travel experiences into lasting memories filled with joy, laughter, and companionship.

2.6 The Art of Letter Writing: Keeping Connections Alive

In an era dominated by instant digital communication, the art of letter writing holds a special kind of magic. Each handwritten letter carries not only the words but also the personal touch of its sender, making it a deeply emotional and meaningful form of communication. The act of sitting down to write a letter requires a level of thoughtfulness and presence that electronic messages often lack. This personal touch can significantly impact the recipient, providing a tangible connection that feels both nostalgic and profound.

When you write a letter, you infuse it with your personality, from your handwriting and choice of paper to the way you seal the envelope. This personal expression allows you to share a part of yourself in a way that text messages and emails cannot replicate. The physical nature of letters also gives them a sense of permanence and importance, making them cherished keepsakes that can be held, stored, and revisited over the years. For retirees, who often value the preservation of memories and relationships, this aspect of letter writing can be particularly appealing.

Starting the practice of letter writing can be a delightful endeavor. Begin by selecting stationery that reflects your personality or the message you wish to convey. Whether it's classic and elegant or colorful and whimsical, your choice of paper and envelope can set the tone for your message. Next, consider investing in a good pen that makes writing a pleasure. The physical act of writing should feel comfortable and enjoyable, encouraging you to pen your thoughts freely.

Finding pen pals might seem like a challenge initially, but numerous communities and websites are dedicated to reviving this beautiful art form. You can connect with people across the globe who share similar interests or life experiences, broadening your perspective and enriching your social circle. Alternatively, consider writing to family members or long-lost friends. A surprise letter can rekindle old relationships and create a bridge to new conversations. Include updates about your life, inquire about theirs, and perhaps share a memory or a piece of advice, making each letter a meaningful exchange.

The Joy of Receiving Mail

The anticipation of receiving mail adds an element of joy and surprise to everyday life. There's something inherently exciting about seeing an envelope with your name handwritten on it among the usual stack of bills and advertisements. This anticipation builds a sense of connection and continuity with the sender, making the eventual reading of the letter a significant moment of your day. Unlike the fleeting nature of digital messages, the deliberate pace of postal mail adds a rhythm to your relationships that is both calming and satisfying.

This joy is not limited to the content of the letters but extends to the entire experience of receiving and reading them. The ritual of sitting down with a cup of tea to read a letter, feeling the texture of the paper, and absorbing the words at your own pace is a profoundly satisfying experience. It's a personal interaction that stands in stark contrast to the impersonal nature of scrolling through a newsfeed or inbox. Each letter becomes a moment of connection that enriches your day, deepening your appreciation for the relationships that matter in your life.

Preserving Relationships

Regular letter writing can strengthen and preserve relationships over distances that might otherwise weaken with time and separation. Letters allow you to share in-depth reflections, personal stories, and heartfelt emotions that might not come through in everyday digital communication. This depth of sharing fosters a strong emotional bond between you and the recipient, grounding your relationship in shared experiences and mutual understanding.

Moreover, the act of writing letters can be a reflective practice, helping you articulate thoughts and feelings that you might not express in face-to-face conversations or quick phone calls. This introspection not only clarifies your own feelings but also enhances the quality of communication with your correspondents, making each interaction more meaningful. As these letters accumulate over time, they create a written legacy of your relationships, chronicling your connections and the growth they have nurtured in your life and the lives of others.

In embracing the art of letter writing, you engage in a practice that enriches your life with depth, reflection, and enduring connections. This chapter has explored how reviving personal correspondence can transform your relationships and enhance your daily life, providing joy, anticipation, and a profound sense of connection. As we close this chapter, remember that each letter you write or receive weaves a stronger thread in the fabric of your relationships, preserving bonds that might otherwise be lost in the fast-paced digital world.

Moving forward, the next chapter will explore new dimensions of personal growth and community engagement, building on the foundations laid here. You'll discover how continuing education, volunteer work, and cultural participation can further enrich your retirement experience, offering new avenues for learning, giving, and belonging.

Interactive Elements: Staying Connected

Lay the foundations for these new connections by writing these down

- Local and online groups
- Friends on social media
- Themed gatherings
- Local Community events
- Opportunities for Group Travel
- Who can you write letters to?

3. Embracing Technology in Retirement

In the golden years of retirement, technology emerges not just as a modern convenience, but as a gateway to a world brimming with possibilities. Picture this: a Sunday morning where you wake up not to the ringing of an old alarm clock, but to the gentle tones of a smart device, reminding you of a video call with your grandchildren scheduled right after breakfast. Or consider a quiet afternoon turning into an intellectually stimulating discussion with peers from around the globe, right from the comfort of your living room. These scenarios are not snippets from a futuristic film but are realities made possible by the adept use of tablets, smartphones, and the myriad of applications they support. Embracing technology in retirement can transform the way you connect, learn, and enjoy your leisure time, making every day both manageable and exciting.

3.1 Tablets and Smartphones: A Beginner's Guide for Retirees

Device Selection Tips

First of all, you need to select the right tools. Start by considering what it is you want to do with your device. You may want a larger screen to enable you to read or browse easily like a tablet or you may prefer to have something smaller and more mobile like a smartphone. If you expect to use it for long periods of time for extended reading sessions or video calls with family, then pick one with longer battery durability.

Then you choose the operating system. Do you prefer Android or an Apple device like an iPhone? Each has its own interface and set of features. If you are unsure, then the best thing is to visit a local electronics store and speak to the experts. Tell them what you want to use it for and they can show you different models and you can even get hands on experience with the different models to get an idea of which you would prefer to use. The sales representatives can provide demonstrations and guide you through the basic features of each device.

Basic Operations

Once you select your device, mastering its basic operations is your next step. This journey begins the moment you power on the device. Take the time to familiarize yourself with the home screen, where you'll find all your apps and tools. Navigating to settings will allow you to adjust such essentials as font size—a particularly useful feature for those who find smaller text challenging to read—and screen brightness. Don't be afraid to ask those very same sales representatives who sold you the device to help you set it up.

Installing applications is another fundamental skill. App stores on both Android and iPhone are repositories of countless apps designed to make life easier and more enjoyable. Start with the essentials: a good browser, a few social media apps, perhaps a news app, and some security software to keep your device safe. Learning to download and update apps ensures that you always have access to the latest features and security enhancements. Depending on how much you are already familiar with these devices this will be either straightforward or daunting. There are courses out there in local communities that help the older generations to get used to new technology or if you have family or friends already familiar with the use of apps then enlist their help.

Staying Connected

The true power of tablets and smartphones lies in their ability to keep you connected with friends and family, no matter the distance. Messaging apps like WhatsApp or social media platforms such as Facebook provide instant communication channels. Most of these apps are free and user-friendly, offering not just text messaging but also voice messages and video calls. Taking the time to set up a profile and adding your contacts can open new doors to daily interactions that keep loneliness at bay and your social network vibrant.

Moreover, these devices can help maintain and organize social engagements. Utilizing calendar apps to set reminders for birthdays, anniversaries, or coffee dates ensures that you never miss an important occasion. The convenience of having all your social commitments in one place, accessible at the touch of a button, simplifies your social management remarkably.

Lifelong Learning

Beyond communication, tablets and smartphones are windows to knowledge and continuous learning. Numerous educational apps cater to a wide array of interests and are specifically designed with user-friendly interfaces for all ages. Apps like Duolingo for language learning, or Coursera and Khan Academy for a range of courses from science to the arts, provide retirees with the tools to expand their knowledge and skills at their own pace.

For those interested in less formal learning experiences, podcasts and educational videos on platforms like YouTube offer a wealth of information on nearly any topic imaginable. Whether it's learning a new skill, staying updated with current events, or exploring hobbies, these resources transform your device into a classroom of your choice.

~

Interactive Element: Educational Apps Checklist

To help you get started on your journey of lifelong learning through technology, here's a checklist of educational apps to explore:

- **For Languages:** Duolingo, Babbel
- **For Academic Courses:** Coursera, edX, Khan Academy
- **For Skill Building:** Udemy, LinkedIn Learning

- **For Leisure Learning:** TED Talks, YouTube

This checklist offers a starting point for you to explore the vast educational opportunities that your device provides, ensuring that your retirement is not just a time of leisure but also of intellectual growth and exploration.

∽

As you delve into the world of tablets and smartphones, each swipe and tap brings you closer to a broader world of connections and knowledge. These devices are not just tools; they are portals to an enriched, engaged, and energetic retirement. Embrace them with curiosity and an open mind, and you will discover that technology is indeed one of the most empowering tools at your disposal in the modern age.

3.2 Exploring the World of Social Media Safely and Enjoyably

Social media, when navigated wisely, can become an enriching part of your retirement, allowing you to stay engaged with the world and your interests. The first step in this digital adventure is selecting the right platforms that align with your interests and social preferences. Each social media platform has its unique flair and user base, which can significantly influence your online experience. For instance, if your interest lies in visual arts or crafts, Instagram or Pinterest could be your canvas, showcasing and discovering visual inspirations. Conversely, if you enjoy engaging in discussions or staying updated with news and contemporary issues, platforms like Twitter or Facebook might suit you better. These platforms allow for real-time engagement with global events and community discussions. It is also beneficial to consider the demographic that each platform attracts; some are favored by younger audiences, while others have a more mature user base. Understanding where you might find like-minded peers can enhance your social interaction online.

Once you have chosen a platform that feels right, the next crucial step is to ensure your privacy and safety online. Navigating privacy settings might seem daunting at first, but taking the time to understand these can protect you from potential online risks. Start by accessing the privacy settings section on your chosen platform; this is usually found in the account or settings menu. Here, you can control who sees your posts, who can contact you, and manage other security settings like two-factor authentication, which adds an extra layer of security to your account. It's advisable to restrict your posts' visibility to people you trust or to friends-only, especially if you are sharing personal information or photos. Regularly updating your privacy settings, along with your password, can safeguard your account against unauthorized access and ensure your online interactions remain secure.

Engaging content creation is an exciting aspect of social media that allows you to share your life's joys and interests with others. Whether it's posting about a new hobby, sharing a recipe, or recounting tales from past travels, your content can inspire and connect you with others who share similar interests. When creating content, consider what you enjoy and think about what others might find interesting or helpful. Photos and videos often make posts more engaging, but ensure that any visuals you share are ones you are comfortable with others seeing. Writing with authentic voice invites more genuine interactions and can lead to meaningful exchanges in the comments section of your posts. Additionally, using hashtags relevant to your content can increase its visibility, helping you reach a broader audience who shares your interests.

Connecting with like-minded individuals is perhaps one of the most rewarding aspects of social media. To find groups or communities that align with your hobbies or interests, use the search function on the social media platforms. Most platforms have interest-based groups where members share information, ask questions, and support each other. Whether you are a gardening enthusiast, a book lover, or a technology geek, there is likely a group waiting for you. Joining these groups can not only provide a sense of belonging but also offer a platform for learning and sharing knowledge. Engage actively within these communities by commenting on posts, asking questions, and sharing your experiences. Over time, these digital interactions can lead to friendships and a support network that enhances your social life, both online and offline.

As you delve deeper into the world of social media, remember that this digital journey is yours to shape. Choose platforms that match your lifestyle, safeguard your privacy, create content that reflects your personality, and connect with communities that enrich your experience. Through thoughtful engagement, you can transform social media from a simple pastime into a vibrant part of your daily life, filled with learning, sharing, and connecting.

3.3 Video Calling: Staying Visually Connected with Family and Friends

In an era where geographical distances are increasingly trivialized by technology, video calling stands out as a remarkable tool that not only bridges miles but also brings the comforting nuances of face-to-face interaction into your living room. Whether it's witnessing the infectious laughter of your grandchildren or watching the subtle expressions of an old friend as you recount shared memories, video calls add a rich layer of connection that voice calls or text messages simply cannot match. For retirees, mastering video calling means turning any day into an opportunity for meaningful interaction, making it essential to select the right app and understand its setup and usage.

When it comes to choosing a video calling app, several popular options cater well to the needs and preferences of retirees. Skype, a long-time favorite, offers robust functionality with the ability to make video calls, send messages, and even share files. Its interface is relatively straightforward, making it suitable for those who may not be very tech-savvy. Another excellent choice is Zoom, which has gained immense popularity for its high-quality video and ability to host multiple participants effortlessly, ideal for family gatherings or group meetings with friends. For Apple device users, FaceTime provides a seamless and integrated video calling experience, with the added benefit of exceptional video and audio quality. Each of these platforms has its merits, and your choice might depend on factors like the devices you and your family members use, the level of security each platform offers, and how intuitive you find the user interface.

Setting up for your first video call might seem daunting, but it's quite straightforward once you break it down into steps. Begin by installing your chosen application from the app store available on your device. Once installed, you'll need to create an account, typically requiring an email address and a password. After logging in, take a moment to explore the app's interface. Familiarize yourself with where the contacts section is, how to answer a call, and where the settings are. Before making your first call, ensure your device is connected to a stable internet connection to avoid any disruptions during the call. Test your camera and microphone through the app's settings; this is crucial as it ensures that you can be seen and heard clearly. If the video or audio quality is poor, checking your device's settings to make sure the right camera and microphone are selected could resolve the issue. Once everything is set up, you're ready to make your first call. Simply select a contact from your list and press the video call button—within seconds, you should be connected and ready to enjoy a real-time conversation.

For many, the initial hesitation with video technology stems from unfamiliarity with the devices or fear of pressing the wrong button. Overcoming these technological hesitations begins with patience and practice. Start by making regular video calls to family members or friends who can guide you through the process. As you become more familiar with the functionalities, your confidence will naturally grow. Don't hesitate to use the help and support features provided by most apps or consider asking a family member to walk you through the process in person or over the phone. Remember, each attempt brings you closer to mastering this valuable communication tool.

Regular video call gatherings, such as virtual family reunions or weekly catch-ups with friends, can be an excellent way to maintain strong relationships despite physical distance. Organizing these gatherings requires a bit of coordination but the effort is well worth it. Choose a regular time and day that works for most people to ensure maximum participation. For larger gatherings, apps like Zoom or Microsoft Teams are ideal as they can accommodate multiple participants simultaneously and offer features like 'Rooms' where groups can split into smaller, more intimate conversations. During festive seasons or special occasions like birthdays or anniversaries, make these video calls a tradition. Themed virtual parties, where everyone might wear a festive hat or share a meal over the call, can add an element of fun and celebration to the gathering.

3.4 Online Courses and Workshops for Lifelong Learning

The digital age has revolutionized access to education, making lifelong learning not just a possibility but a delightful reality for many retirees. With an array of online courses and workshops available at your fingertips, the challenge often lies not in finding opportunities to learn but in selecting the ones that best match your interests, lifestyle, and existing skills. Embarking on this educational adventure begins with identifying what you wish to learn or explore further. Perhaps you have a longstanding interest in history or a newfound curiosity about digital photography. Maybe you're considering a deeper understanding of nutrition to enhance your health, or you're intrigued by creative writing. Websites like Udemy, Coursera, and MasterClass offer courses in virtually every subject imaginable, taught by industry experts and academics. To find courses that align with your interests, start by browsing these platforms using their detailed search and filter options, which can help you narrow down choices by subject, difficulty level, and even course duration.

Consider your current skill level and how much time you can realistically dedicate to learning. If you're a beginner, look for introductory courses that start with the basics and are structured to support first-time learners. For more advanced topics or if you're building on existing knowledge, intermediate or expert-level courses can offer more depth and challenge. It's also worth noting the format of the course—some people prefer structured classes with regular video lectures and assignments, while others might enjoy more flexible courses that allow you to learn at your own pace. Checking reviews and ratings by other students can also provide insights into the course's effectiveness and can help you make an informed decision.

The benefits of engaging in online learning are manifold. One of the most significant advantages is the flexibility it offers. Unlike traditional classroom settings, online courses allow you to learn from anywhere at any time. You can study from the comfort of your home, at a local café, or even while traveling, making it easy to integrate learning into your daily routine without the need to commute or adhere to a strict schedule. This flexibility is particularly beneficial for retirees who manage multiple interests or health considerations. Furthermore, the range of courses available online is vast; you can learn everything from quantum physics to basket weaving. This variety ensures that no matter what piques your interest, there's likely a course available, providing you the freedom to explore diverse subjects at your own pace.

Engaging effectively with online learning communities can significantly enhance your educational experience. Most online courses offer discussion forums or platforms where you can interact with fellow learners and instructors. These forums are invaluable for gaining deeper insights into the topics discussed, sharing your own knowledge and experiences, and receiving feedback on any assignments or projects. Active participation in these communities can also help you feel more connected and motivated. Ask questions, offer answers, and share resources. Some courses also provide opportunities for group projects or peer reviews, offering a more interactive learning experience that can mimic the dynamics of a traditional classroom. Engaging with peers not only enriches your learning but can also lead to friendships and professional connections that transcend the virtual classroom.

Setting achievable learning goals is crucial for maintaining motivation and ensuring that your educational pursuits yield tangible results. Begin by defining clear, specific goals for what you want to achieve through each course or workshop. These could range from mastering a particular skill, such as photo editing, to gaining a comprehensive understanding of a broader subject like World History. Break these larger goals into smaller, manageable tasks such as completing one module per week or dedicating fifteen minutes a day to studying. This approach helps prevent feeling overwhelmed and keeps you progressing steadily towards your larger goals. Additionally, integrate your learning activities into your daily or weekly schedule. Just as you might set aside time for physical exercise or social outings, allocate regular time slots for your educational activities. This not only helps in forming a routine but also signals to your brain that this activity is a priority, enhancing your focus and retention during study times.

As you navigate through the vast landscape of online learning, remember that each course you take not only adds to your knowledge base but also keeps your mind active and engaged. Whether you're looking to delve into academic subjects, pick up new hobbies, or connect with like-minded learners, the world of online courses and workshops offers a flexible, diverse, and enriching way to embrace lifelong learning in retirement.

3.5 Discovering New Music and Podcasts

The digital age brings with it an unprecedented access to music and spoken word content through streaming services and podcasts, making it easier than ever to explore a vast universe of sounds and stories. For retirees, this accessibility opens up delightful avenues for entertainment, learning, and relaxation, all tailored to personal tastes and moods. Navigating music streaming services begins with selecting a platform that aligns with your preferences and needs. Popular services like Spotify, Apple Music, and Amazon Music offer extensive libraries of music spanning all genres and eras. These platforms typically provide a free version with advertisements or a premium subscription that offers additional features such as offline listening and ad-free streaming. Start by exploring these platforms through their free trials to determine which interface you find most user-friendly and which service offers the music selections that best match your tastes.

Once you have chosen a service, the next step is to learn how to effectively use it. These platforms are designed with user-friendly interfaces that make it easy to search for specific artists, albums, or songs. Moreover, they offer curated playlists that can introduce you to new music based on your listening habits and preferences. Take advantage of these features by exploring different genres and artists, allowing the algorithm to refine its suggestions for you. This exploration can be particularly enjoyable, leading you to discover music that you might not have encountered otherwise. Additionally, most services offer the ability to create your own playlists, giving you the freedom to compile collections of your favorite songs or organize music by mood, occasion, or activity.

Finding podcasts that entertain, inform, or cater to specific interests has also become an engaging pursuit for many retirees. Podcasts cover an astonishing range of topics, from history and science to health and hobbies. Platforms like Apple Podcasts, Spotify, and Google Podcasts are rich resources, hosting podcasts from around the world. Start by identifying topics that intrigue you and search for podcasts in those categories. The beauty of podcasts lies in their diversity; whether you want to dive deep into political discussions, get lost in a storytelling session, or learn more about gardening tips, there's likely a podcast that covers these subjects. Many podcast platforms also offer recommendations based on the shows you listen to, making it easier to discover new content that aligns with your interests.

Creating personal playlists for various moods and activities can enhance how you experience music and podcasts. Consider compiling a playlist of calming music for relaxation, an upbeat collection for exercise, or a selection of educational podcasts for your morning coffee routine. These personalized playlists ensure that you always have the perfect backdrop for any part of your day. The process of creating these playlists can be quite intuitive on most streaming services. You typically select your favorite tracks or episodes and add them to a new playlist, which you can name and customize at your leisure. This customization not only allows you to organize your listening experience but also makes it easy to return to your favorite content whenever you wish.

Sharing music and podcast recommendations with friends and family can also be a wonderful way to connect and enrich your relationships. When you discover a song that moves you or a podcast episode that inspires you, sharing it with others can lead to meaningful conversations and shared experiences. Most streaming platforms make it easy to share content via social media, email, or direct links. This act of sharing not only helps you stay connected with loved ones but can also introduce them to new music and ideas, fostering a shared auditory landscape that can be discussed and enjoyed together. Whether it's reminiscing over classic hits with old friends or exploring new genres with your grandchildren, the shared experience of music and podcasts can bridge generations and strengthen bonds, making each discovery a chance to learn more about yourself and the people in your life.

3.6 Blogging About Your Retirement Journey

In the vibrant landscape of retirement, starting a personal blog offers a unique platform to document and share your experiences, insights, and adventures. This digital journal not only serves as a repository of your memories but also connects you with a community of readers who can find inspiration and companionship in your posts. The process of setting up your blog is simpler than you might think. Platforms like WordPress, Blogger, or Medium offer user-friendly interfaces that cater to individuals who might not have extensive technical expertise. Start by choosing a blogging platform that aligns with your needs—consider factors such as ease of use, customization options, and the potential for audience engagement. Once you've selected a platform, setting up your blog typically involves creating an account, selecting a blog template that reflects your style, and customizing it to suit your taste. Most platforms provide a range of templates that you can personalize with your choice of colors, fonts, and layout styles.

Creating compelling content is the heart of blogging. Your retirement journey offers a treasure trove of topics that can engage and inspire your audience. For example, travel diaries provide a wonderful way to share your adventures with readers, detailing the places you've visited, the cultures you've experienced, and the people you've met. Each post can be rich with photos and anecdotes that bring your travels to life for your readers. If you have a hobby like gardening, cooking, or crafting, consider creating tutorials that share your knowledge and expertise. Step-by-step guides on planting a seasonal garden, recipes for your favorite dishes, or instructions for a craft project not only provide valuable content for your readers but also position you as an expert in your hobby area.

Connecting with your readers is crucial for growing your blog's audience and enhancing reader engagement. Encourage your readers to comment on your posts by asking questions or inviting opinions at the end of each blog entry. Respond to comments with thoughtful replies that foster a conversation. This interaction helps build a community around your blog, keeping readers coming back for more and sharing your posts with others. Additionally, consider integrating social media to broaden your blog's reach. Sharing your posts on Facebook, Twitter, or Pinterest can attract new readers who might be interested in your topics. Regularly updating your blog with new posts keeps your audience engaged and helps maintain a steady flow of traffic to your blog. If you prefer to just keep friends and family up to date with your adventures, creating a Whatsapp group which only allows you as the administrator to post is a good option.

The therapeutic benefits of blogging are profound. Writing about your experiences can be a cathartic activity, helping you to reflect on your life and articulate your thoughts and feelings. This reflection can contribute significantly to your mental and emotional well-being, providing a sense of purpose and a means to express yourself creatively. Moreover, blogging allows you to leave behind a digital legacy that can be cherished by family and friends for years to come. Your blog becomes a personalized narrative of your retirement journey, capturing your adventures, achievements, and growth during this significant phase of your life.

As this chapter concludes, we reflect on how technology—from tablets and smartphones to social media and blogging—plays a pivotal role in enriching your retirement experience. Embracing these digital tools opens up new avenues for connection, learning, and self-expression, making your retirement years as engaging and fulfilling as any other phase of your life. As we transition from exploring the digital world to discovering physical activities and hobbies in the next chapter, remember that the integration of technology in your daily life can significantly enhance these experiences, bringing ease and joy to your leisure activities and pursuits.

Embracing Technology in Retirement

Gill spent a long and fulfilling career in the public sector, starting as a nurse and social worker, and ultimately working as a social worker where she specialized in the fostering. When she retired at 62, she wanted to maintain a connection to her professional roots, so she continues to serve on a foster care panel every few months. This role keeps her social worker registration current and allows her to stay engaged with her past work life.

A passionate walker, Gill frequently embarks on walking trips, ranging from a few days to a week. She relishes countryside walks with her daughter and more distant adventures with friends. To stay active, she regularly hits the gym and plays padel tennis. In her retirement, she has embraced various volunteer roles, working for a charity for those who are terminally ill and is volunteering for a charity shop. Her next volunteering endeavor is in bereavement counseling, for which she is currently undergoing training.

Meetups have been a social lifeline for Gill, introducing her to a host of new friends. With these friends, she enjoys playing padel and attending various social events, including a supper club that explores new restaurants each month.

Finding purpose in retirement is crucial for Gill, and she has applied to a three-year counseling course that will qualify her to take on clients. This course, which meets one morning a week, allows her the flexibility to balance her other activities. With her pension providing financial security, any income from clients will be a bonus.

Travel is another of Gill's passions. In the past year, she has enjoyed a cruise and visited friends across the country, making good use of her senior rail card for discounted travel. With her active lifestyle and diverse interests, Gill continues to lead a vibrant and purposeful life in retirement.

4. Health, Fitness, and Well-Being

I magine waking up each morning not with aches and pains but with a new feeling of serenity and vitality. An integrated practice of yoga and meditation can turn this vision into a reality and help you maintain your physical and mental health through retirement. You may be imagining headstands and difficult positions and think that is too much for you but in reality, these practices can suit all levels depending on age and mobility level.

See them as transformative practices to increase your health and wellbeing.

4.1 Yoga and Meditation for Every Body

Adaptable Practices

Yoga and meditation practices have their roots in ancient traditions and nowadays have evolved into practices everyone can enjoy. They can be modified very easily to cater to various mobility levels and physical conditions ensuring that everyone can benefit, from the most agile to those with physical limitations. Flexibility is important in later life and chair yoga, for example, modifies traditional yoga practices so that they can be performed while seated, without having to leave your chair, ideal for those with mobility issues or balance issues. Meditation too can be performed anywhere; seated or lying down or even when walking.

Start by identifying your current physical condition and any specific needs to have. It is useful to consult either a health professional or a certified yoga instructor who can advise on what type of modifications you would need. They can help put together a practice which takes into account your own body's needs, making you able to practice safely and effectively. There are many beginners' yoga classes that focus on gentle yoga and guided meditation which are designed to introduce you to the fundamental principles of the practice in a supportive environment where you can go at your own pace. Many community centers and local gyms offer such classes for older adults which will introduce you to a community of your peers with similar physical concerns and fitness goals.

Mental Health Benefits

The mental health benefits of regular yoga and meditation are profound. Engaging in these practices can lead to significant improvements in mental clarity, stress reduction, and overall emotional well-being. Meditation, by encouraging deep breathing and mindfulness, helps regulate the body's stress response, reducing the prevalence of stress-related hormones in the bloodstream. This regulation not only helps in managing day-to-day stress but also enhances your overall mood and outlook on life. Yoga complements these benefits by combining physical postures with breathwork, which not only improves physical strength and flexibility but also promotes mental focus and calmness.

The rhythmic breathing and mindful awareness cultivated through these practices are particularly effective in managing anxiety and depression, common concerns in retirement. The meditative aspect of yoga, known as pranayama, teaches you to control your breathing, which can help manage and reduce moments of anxiety. Regular practice can lead to a greater sense of control over your emotions and a deeper sense of peace throughout your daily activities.

Community Classes vs. Home Practice

Deciding between joining a community class or practicing at home presents a set of pros and cons that you should consider based on your personal preferences and lifestyle. Community classes offer the advantage of professional guidance from certified instructors who can ensure you are performing movements safely and effectively. These classes also provide the opportunity to meet and interact with peers, which can be incredibly motivating and enriching. The structured setting of a community class can help you maintain a regular schedule, which is crucial for developing a consistent practice.

On the other hand, practicing at home offers flexibility and convenience, especially if you have limited mobility or prefer a more private setting. Online resources like instructional videos, virtual classes, and guided meditation apps can provide significant support for home practice. These resources allow you to tailor your practice to your schedule and preferences, often at a lower cost than in-person classes. However, the key to successful home practice is self-motivation; setting regular times for your practice and creating a dedicated space for yoga and meditation can help maintain discipline.

Getting Started

Embarking on the path of yoga and meditation requires minimal equipment, making it an accessible option for most retirees. For yoga, basic props include a yoga mat, which provides cushioning and traction, and may include blocks or a strap to aid in performing certain poses. Choosing the right mat—thicker mats offer more cushioning, which can be beneficial for those with joint issues—is essential for comfort and safety. For meditation, a comfortable cushion or chair can help in maintaining a proper and comfortable posture.

Finding the right instructor or class is crucial when you're just starting out. Look for instructors who are experienced in teaching older adults or who are knowledgeable about modifications for various physical conditions. Many yoga studios and community centers offer trial classes, which can be a great way to find an instructor and a class style that suits your needs. Additionally, setting realistic goals for your practice can help keep you motivated and engaged. Start with short sessions, perhaps 15 to 20 minutes, and gradually increase the duration as your body adjusts and your interest develops. Always remember, the journey into yoga and meditation is personal and should be approached at your own pace, with your comfort and safety as priorities.

As you incorporate yoga and meditation into your routine, you will likely notice enhancements not just in your physical health but in your overall disposition towards life's challenges. Each stretch, each breath brings you closer to a state of balance and peace, proving that true well-being is a harmonious blend of mind, body, and spirit.

4.2 Walking Clubs: Socializing While Staying Fit

Initiating or becoming part of a walking club can be an excellent way for retirees to maintain both social and physical fitness routines. If you're considering starting a walking club, the first step is to gauge interest among your community, friends, or neighbors. A simple notice on community bulletin boards, social media groups, or a local community center can attract others who share your enthusiasm. When forming a club, consider setting a regular schedule, such as weekly walks, and plan routes that are convenient and accessible for all members. Consider varying the locations to keep the walks interesting; parks, nature trails, and different neighborhoods can provide refreshing environments that enhance the experience. For those looking to join an existing group, local fitness clubs, community centers, and senior centers often sponsor walking clubs. Websites and apps dedicated to fitness and outdoor activities can also connect you with nearby walking groups.

The health benefits of regular walking are vast and particularly impactful for retirees. Physiologically, walking is a stellar cardiovascular exercise that strengthens the heart and lungs, improving overall endurance. This activity helps manage weight, reduces the risk of heart disease, and lowers blood pressure. Importantly for many at this stage of life, walking enhances mobility and flexibility, which are crucial for maintaining independence. The rhythmic nature of walking also promotes joint health by lubricating joints and strengthening the muscles that support them. Beyond these physical benefits, walking has significant mental health advantages. Regular walking, especially in natural settings, can reduce stress, anxiety, and depression. The act of moving outdoors not only diverts the mind from daily worries but also stimulates the production of endorphins, the body's natural mood elevators.

Socializing while walking can transform this solitary exercise into a vibrant social activity that fosters friendships and accountability. Walking with a group provides a social stimulus that can make physical activity more enjoyable and motivate you to stick with a regular exercise routine. The social interactions experienced during these outings can also lead to stronger, more supportive relationships. To enhance the social aspect, you might incorporate themes or challenges into your walks, like bird watching, historical tours of your town, or photography challenges that encourage members to capture images of their surroundings during the walk. These activities add an element of fun and engagement, keeping the group dynamic lively and interesting. Additionally, setting group goals, such as participating in a charity walk or reaching a collective mileage goal, can foster a sense of team spirit and shared purpose.

Safety and accessibility should always be top priorities to ensure that walks are enjoyable and inclusive for all participants. When planning routes, consider the varying mobility levels within your group. Opt for paths that are well-maintained and free of obstacles that could pose tripping hazards. Ensure that the routes are well-lit, particularly if you are walking during early mornings or late evenings. It's also wise to check the weather forecast before setting out and to advise members to wear suitable clothing and footwear for the conditions. For those with significant mobility limitations, consider organizing shorter routes or having designated resting spots along the way. Always have a first aid kit handy and ensure at least one member of the group is familiar with basic first aid practices. Additionally, it's beneficial for the group to have a way to communicate with each other easily, like mobile phones or walkie-talkies, especially on more secluded trails.

By integrating these elements into the structure and operation of a walking club, you create a safe, enjoyable, and health-promoting activity that enhances the quality of life for its members. Walking becomes more than mere physical exercise; it evolves into a shared endeavor that fosters health, happiness, and a vibrant sense of community among its participants.

4.3 Aquatic Exercises for Joint-Friendly Fitness

The buoyancy of water offers a unique environment that greatly reduces the strain on your joints while providing resistance that helps strengthen muscles and improve cardiovascular health. This natural characteristic of water makes aquatic exercises especially beneficial for joint health and pain reduction. When submerged, your body bears less weight, which significantly decreases the pressure on weight-bearing joints like hips, knees, and the spine. This reduction in joint stress is particularly advantageous if you suffer from arthritis or other forms of joint pain. Furthermore, the resistance of water makes every movement a gentle strength training exercise, helping to build muscle mass and bone density, which are crucial for maintaining mobility and reducing the risk of osteoporosis.

Water's viscosity provides a natural resistance that requires more effort to move through compared to air. This resistance is evenly distributed, which means it can help improve overall muscle tone and endurance without the risk of injury from weights or high-impact activities. Additionally, the cooling effect of water can make exercising a more comfortable and enjoyable experience, particularly if you are sensitive to heat or prone to overheating during physical activity. Engaging in regular aquatic exercises can lead to improvements in your cardiovascular stamina, muscular strength, and flexibility, all of which contribute to better overall health and a decreased risk of chronic diseases such as type 2 diabetes and heart disease.

Introducing yourself to a variety of water-based exercises can keep your routine enjoyable and challenging. Swimming is perhaps the most well-known aquatic exercise and serves as an excellent full-body workout. However, if swimming laps isn't appealing or feasible due to skill level, there are plenty of other options that can provide similar benefits. Water aerobics, for example, includes a range of movements and exercises that are performed in a vertical position in shallow water. These might include leg lifts, standing water push-ups, and dance-like movements, all choreographed to music which adds an element of fun and can enhance your coordination and balance.

Another option is water walking or jogging, which simply involves walking or jogging in the water, usually in the shallow end of a pool. This activity increases heart rate and circulation, and you can adjust the intensity by altering your speed or the depth of the water. For those looking for a challenge, aquatic resistance tools like water weights or noodles can be used to increase resistance and help build muscle strength. Each of these activities can be modified to suit your fitness level and goals, making water exercises a versatile option for maintaining fitness in retirement.

Finding a local pool that offers senior-friendly exercise classes might seem daunting, but many community centers, gyms, and public pools now recognize the growing demand for such activities and offer programs specifically designed for older adults. Start by checking with local community centers or public pools about the availability of aquatic exercise classes. These facilities often provide a range of options from gentle water yoga to more energetic water aerobics. Additionally, many YMCAs, fitness clubs, and senior centers offer specialized classes that focus on joint health and mobility improvements.

When exploring these options, don't hesitate to ask about the qualifications of the instructors and whether the classes are designed to accommodate various mobility levels and health conditions. It's also worth asking other participants about their experiences with the classes to gauge if it might be a good fit for you. If you prefer a more personalized approach or require specific accommodations, some facilities offer one-on-one sessions with trained aquatic therapists or instructors who can tailor a program to your specific needs.

Starting an aquatic exercise routine safely involves several considerations to ensure that you not only enjoy your time in the water but also benefit from it without risk. Before beginning any new exercise regimen, it's advisable to consult with your healthcare provider, especially if you have existing health issues or concerns. Once you have the green light, the next step is to acquire the appropriate gear. Non-slip water shoes can enhance safety by preventing falls on wet surfaces. A comfortable, well-fitting swimsuit and a water bottle for hydration are also essential.

When you first start, take it slow. Begin with sessions that are easy on your body, gradually increasing the duration and intensity of your workouts as your fitness improves. Pay attention to how your body responds during and after exercises and adjust your activities accordingly. It's also beneficial to warm up before entering the pool and to cool down afterwards, just as you would with land-based exercises. These practices help prevent muscle strains and other injuries. Joining a class can be particularly helpful when starting out, as instructors can ensure that you perform exercises correctly and safely, providing guidance tailored to your fitness level and health status.

As you integrate aquatic exercises into your routine, you may find that the water not only supports your body but also uplifts your spirit. The soothing nature of water, combined with the physical benefits of the exercises, can greatly enhance your quality of life, making each session something to look forward to.

Before we go onto the health and wellbeing of your mind, don't rule out other sports. Of course, this will depend on your own fitness levels but it may be that you fancy trying the archetypical retirement game golf or having a go at the fastest growing sport padel tennis.

4.4 Brain Games to Keep Your Mind Sharp

In the realm of maintaining and enhancing cognitive function as we age; brain games offer a delightful and effective strategy. These activities are not merely pastimes but essential tools that stimulate mental activity and can help fortify the mind against the natural cognitive decline associated with aging. Engaging regularly in brain games can enhance various aspects of cognitive function, including memory, problem-solving skills, and processing speed. The mechanics of these games often require critical thinking, pattern recognition, and strategic planning, which are all exercises for the brain, keeping it active and agile. This mental exercise is akin to how physical exercise benefits the body, promoting overall brain health and maintaining cognitive functions that might otherwise wane as we grow older.

Among the plethora of brain games suited for retirees, certain types stand out for their accessibility and cognitive benefits. Crossword puzzles and Sudoku are classic examples that challenge language and numerical skills, respectively. These puzzles are readily available in newspapers, books, and online platforms, making them easy to incorporate into your daily routine. For those inclined towards technology, digital platforms offer a wide array of brain games designed specifically to enhance cognitive skills. Apps like Lumosity or CogniFit feature games that are scientifically designed to target specific areas of brain function and offer personalized training routines that adapt to your progress. These platforms also provide feedback and track your improvement over time, adding an extra layer of motivation by allowing you to see tangible progress in your cognitive abilities.

Incorporating these games into your daily life can be both fun and beneficial. Establishing a routine can help make brain training a regular part of your day. Consider setting aside a specific time each day for these activities, perhaps in the morning when your mind is fresh, or as a relaxing evening activity. The key is consistency; just as with physical exercise, regular mental exercise is crucial for reaping the cognitive benefits. Creating a comfortable and quiet space for these activities can enhance your focus and enjoyment. Whether it's a cozy corner of your living room or a spot at your kitchen table with a view, having a designated space can make your brain training sessions something to look forward to each day.

Turning brain gaming into a social activity can also enhance its appeal and effectiveness. Playing games like Scrabble or chess with grandchildren not only allows for cherished bonding time but also introduces a competitive element that can be stimulating and engaging. Consider forming a game club with peers who share your interest in brain games. Meeting regularly to challenge each other in games or puzzles can transform a solitary activity into an enjoyable social event, providing both cognitive stimulation and social interaction. These gatherings can be held in person at a community center or a member's home, or online via video calls, allowing for flexibility in participation. Social interactions during these games provide emotional benefits and can lead to deeper friendships, as you share not only the games but also conversations and experiences.

As you explore the world of brain games, remember that variety is key. Just as with physical activities, varying the types of mental exercises can engage different parts of the brain and prevent monotony. Challenge yourself by trying new games or increasing the difficulty levels of the puzzles you solve. This variety keeps the brain engaged and continuously learning, which is essential for maintaining cognitive health. Whether you're deciphering a complex crossword puzzle, strategizing over a chessboard, or navigating the colorful challenges of a digital brain game, each session is a step toward maintaining a sharp, active mind that enhances your overall quality of life and independence as you age.

4.5 Gardening for Mindfulness and Movement

Embarking on the creation of a garden, regardless of the size of your living space or previous gardening experience, can be a deeply rewarding endeavor that enhances both your physical well-being and mental clarity. To begin, consider what type of garden resonates with your interests and the space available. For those with limited outdoor areas, container gardening offers a versatile solution, enabling you to grow a variety of plants, from flowers to vegetables, on patios, balconies, or even windowsills. Alternatively, vertical gardens are an excellent option for those with minimal floor space, using wall-mounted planters to create a lush green wall. If you have access to a yard or community garden, you have the canvas to create a more traditional garden with rows of vegetables and flower beds.

Starting your garden involves initial planning and preparation. Begin by deciding what you want to grow based on your climate zone, the soil type available, and how much time you can dedicate to garden maintenance. Local gardening centers and online resources can offer guidance on what plants are best suited to your environment. Once you've made your selections, sketch a rough layout of where each plant will go, keeping in mind their light, space, and watering needs. This plan doesn't have to be intricate but should serve as a basic guide to help you start your garden journey. Gathering the necessary tools and materials is the next step. Basics include gardening gloves, a trowel, a watering can or hose, soil, and your chosen plants or seeds. If you're new to gardening, consider starting small—a few pots or a single small bed—to reduce overwhelm as you learn the ropes of plant care.

The act of gardening itself is a physical activity that keeps you moving and engaged. Digging, planting, watering, and weeding are all tasks that involve a range of motions that help improve strength, stamina, and flexibility. The level of activity can be adjusted to your physical abilities, and even an hour a week can have significant health benefits. More than just physical exercise, gardening is an act of nurturing that requires patience and attention, drawing you into the present moment. This mindfulness aspect is one of the key benefits of gardening, as it allows you to focus on the task at hand, away from the distractions and stresses of daily life. The rhythm of gardening tasks, from the repetitive motion of weeding to the focused activity of pruning, can be meditative, helping to clear your mind and reduce stress levels.

Participating in gardening communities, whether locally or online, can enhance your gardening experience by connecting you with like-minded individuals who share your passion for growing things. Local gardening clubs offer the opportunity to meet fellow gardeners, share tips, and even exchange seeds or plants. These clubs often organize workshops or garden tours, which can be a great way to gain new knowledge and inspiration. Online gardening forums and social media groups offer a platform to ask questions, share successes and challenges, and get advice from more experienced gardeners. These communities can be particularly valuable for troubleshooting specific issues like pest problems or soil deficiencies. Engaging with these groups not only broadens your gardening knowledge but also strengthens your social connections, making gardening a shared hobby that fosters community and support.

Therapeutic gardening, a concept that has gained popularity in recent years, refers to the intentional use of gardening activities as a therapeutic tool for improving mental and emotional well-being. This approach is rooted in the idea that regular interaction with nature can have healing effects, helping to alleviate symptoms of stress, depression, and anxiety. Therapeutic gardening can be particularly beneficial in retirement, a period that can sometimes bring feelings of isolation or purposelessness. By focusing on the nurturing aspects of gardening, you actively engage in caring for living things, which can boost mood and self-esteem. Additionally, seeing the tangible results of your efforts, such as a blooming flower or a ripe tomato, can provide a sense of accomplishment and pride. For those interested in exploring therapeutic gardening, many communities offer guided programs that focus on the healing aspects of gardening activities. These programs are often led by trained therapists who specialize in horticultural therapy and can provide structured activities that maximize the therapeutic benefits.

4.6 Healthy Cooking Classes for Fun and Nutrition

Understanding and addressing your nutritional needs is crucial as you navigate through retirement. This phase often brings about significant changes in your body's requirements due to altered metabolism and possibly less physical activity. A diet rich in nutrients can help manage and prevent common age-related conditions such as hypertension, osteoporosis, and heart disease. Therefore, focusing on a balanced diet that includes a variety of fruits, vegetables, lean proteins, and whole grains is essential. Additionally, considering that your caloric needs may decrease, it's important to choose foods that are high in nutrients but not necessarily high in calories. This approach ensures that your body receives all the essential nutrients it needs without the excess calories that can lead to weight gain.

Finding cooking classes that cater to these nutritional needs while also making the process enjoyable can be a delightful way to enhance your culinary skills. Start by searching for local community centers, culinary schools, or even health centers that offer cooking classes focusing on healthy eating or specific dietary needs like diabetic-friendly meals or heart-healthy diets. These classes not only teach you how to prepare delicious and nutritious meals but also often provide valuable information on the nutritional content of different foods and how they benefit your health. For those who prefer the comfort of their home or cannot easily travel, online cooking classes are a fantastic alternative.

Platforms like YouTube have countless tutorials available, and websites dedicated to senior health often feature cooking classes that you can follow along from your kitchen. You could try out new cuisines you have never tried.

Participating in these cooking classes serves more than just educational purposes—it can also be a significant social activity. These classes often bring together people who share a common interest in healthy living and cooking, providing an opportunity to meet new friends or deepen existing relationships. The shared experience of learning to cook something new, coupled with the casual, fun environment of most cooking classes, helps foster a sense of community and belonging. For instance, group activities in these classes, like preparing a meal together, not only make the learning process more interactive but also encourage teamwork and communication, making the entire experience more enjoyable and memorable.

For beginners, the prospect of starting to cook at home, especially if it's something you haven't done much before, might seem daunting. However, with a few simple tips, you can start experimenting with healthy recipes in your own kitchen with confidence. Begin with simple recipes that require basic cooking skills and gradually progress to more complex dishes as your confidence grows. Equip your kitchen with essential tools like a good set of knives, a cutting board, pots, and pans. Having the right tools can make the cooking process smoother and more enjoyable. Start by planning your meals weekly; this not only helps in organizing your shopping list, ensuring you have all the necessary ingredients but also in managing portion sizes and nutritional intake. Choose recipes that can be made in larger batches, which can be refrigerated or frozen for later use, saving you time and effort in the long run.

As you delve into the world of cooking, you'll discover that it's not just about nourishing the body but also about enriching your life with joy and a sense of accomplishment. Each dish you prepare is a testament to your ability to care for yourself and others, a celebration of your commitment to a healthy, fulfilling life. Cooking becomes more than just a task; it transforms into a rewarding activity that feeds both your body and spirit, enhancing your overall well-being.

This chapter has explored various avenues for maintaining and enhancing physical and mental well-being through engaging activities like yoga, walking, aquatic exercises, brain games, gardening, and cooking. Each activity offers unique benefits and opportunities for personal growth, social interaction, and improved health. As you integrate these activities into your life, remember that each step you take, each choice you make, contributes to a richer, more vibrant retirement. Looking forward, the next chapter will delve into exploring hobbies and crafts, expanding on how these creative pursuits can further enhance your quality of life, providing not only pleasure and relaxation but also opportunities for socialization and personal expression. Let the exploration continue as you weave these new activities into the fabric of your daily life, enriching every day with purpose and joy.

Interactive Element: Your health and wellbeing journey

To begin this journey, pick an activity from the ideas below to begin!

- Yoga
- Walking
- Aqua Fitness
- Brain Games
- Gardening
- Cooking and Eating

Make a Difference with Your Review

I have a question for you...

Would you help someone you've never met, even if you never got credit for it?

Who is this person you ask? They are like you. Or, at least, like you used to be. They're stepping into retirement, looking for ways to stay active, make friends, and find joy in this new chapter of life.

Our mission is to make retirement fun, meaningful, and accessible to everyone. Everything I do stems from that mission. And, the only way for me to accomplish that mission is by reaching... well...everyone.

This is where you come in. Most people do, in fact, judge a book by its cover (and its reviews). So here's my ask on behalf of a retiree you've never met:

Please help that retiree by leaving this book a review.

Your gift costs no money and less than 60 seconds to make real, but it can change a fellow retiree's life forever. Your review could help...

...one more retiree find a hobby that brings joy. ...one more grandparent bond with their grandchildren. ...one more person make a new friend. ...one more retiree stay healthy and active. ...one more dream come true.

To get that 'feel good' feeling and help this person for real, all you have to do is...and it takes less than 60 seconds... leave a review.

Simply scan the QR code below to leave your review:

I'm that much more excited to help you enjoy your retirement more than you can possibly imagine. You'll love the activities, tips, and fun ideas I'm about to share in the coming chapters.

Thank you from the bottom of my heart. Now, back to our regularly scheduled program.

- Your biggest fan, Kay Atkinson

P.S. - Fun fact: If you provide something of value to another person, it makes you more valuable to them. If you believe this book will help them, send this book their way.

5. Creative Pursuits and Learning

Whether or not you consider yourself a creative person, now is the time to be a creative person with no pressure to transform it into a moneymaking venture but purely to BE creative. Imagine a blank canvas brimming with potential. With each brush stroke, it becomes an expression of your inner world and a narrative of your life's journey. This activity is not just about adding paint to canvas but it is an exploration of self, tapping into your creative reservoirs and revitalizing your mind. There are so many ways to be creative, to engage in a form of communication that offers a pathway to personal fulfillment and cognitive enrichment.

5.1 Starting Your Artistic Journey: Painting and Drawing

Exploring Different Mediums

The art of painting and drawing offers a plethora of mediums, each with unique characteristics and expressive potentials. For those newly embarking on this artistic journey, the choice of medium can be both exciting and overwhelming. Watercolors, known for their translucent layers, offer a delicate and fluid style, ideal for capturing landscapes or subtle expressions. In contrast, acrylics dry quickly and are versatile, allowing for a range of techniques from thick, textured strokes to diluted washes resembling watercolor effects. Oil paints, celebrated for their rich texture and depth of color, offer a slower drying time, which is perfect for blending and developing detailed artworks over time. Charcoal and graphite, primarily used for drawing, provide a direct and hands-on approach to art-making, excellent for honing observational skills and exploring light and shadow.

Experimenting with different mediums allows you to discover the materials that resonate most deeply with your personal style and artistic intentions. Local art stores often offer small, affordable samples or beginner sets that make this exploration accessible without requiring a significant upfront investment. Engaging with community art groups or online forums can also provide insights and recommendations on navigating the vast choices available, helping you make informed decisions about the materials that will best support your creative endeavors.

Taking Art Classes

Art classes provide structured learning and guidance that can be invaluable when starting your artistic journey. These classes offer a range of benefits, from learning foundational skills and techniques to receiving feedback from experienced instructors and peers. For retirees looking to step into the art world, local community centers, art schools, and galleries often offer classes tailored to beginners, which focus on the basics of drawing and painting and gradually introduce more complex concepts.

When choosing a class, consider the size and focus. Smaller classes allow for more personalized attention from the instructor, which can be crucial as you're mastering new skills. Additionally, many institutions offer themed classes, such as portrait painting, landscape drawing, or abstract art, which can help you focus your learning on areas of specific interest. Participation in these classes not only boosts your artistic skills but also integrates social interactions into your learning process, enriching your experience and providing opportunities to build new friendships with fellow art enthusiasts.

The other popular option these days are one off events, often at local venues such as cafes which offer an evening of art where you are guided through a painting by a teacher. These are for beginners and they are a fantastic way to just get you used to picking up a brush if you haven't done so since your schooldays. They are also a great way to feel the therapy of art, you realize that after a couple of hours painting, you haven't thought about anything else so it is a great relaxer.

The Benefits of Art

Engaging in painting and drawing indeed offers profound mental health benefits, particularly important during retirement. The act of creating art is inherently therapeutic, providing a distraction from everyday worries and reducing stress and anxiety levels. This process of focusing deeply on an artistic endeavor is known as 'flow,' a state of absorption where other concerns seem to recede, providing a sense of peace and well-being.

Moreover, the sense of accomplishment that comes from creating something visually expressive can boost self-esteem and provide a tangible sense of progress, which is especially rewarding. Regularly engaging in artistic activities has been shown to improve cognitive functions by strengthening the connectivity between brain regions, enhancing problem-solving skills, and fostering creative thinking. These cognitive benefits are crucial for maintaining mental agility and can contribute to a more vibrant and fulfilling retirement.

Creating an Art Space

Establishing a personal art space in your home can significantly enhance your artistic practice, providing a designated area where creativity can flourish without interruptions. When setting up this space, consider factors such as lighting, comfort, and accessibility. Natural light is ideal for art-making, so try to locate your space near a window if possible. Equip the area with comfortable seating and sufficient storage for your art supplies, ensuring everything you need is easily accessible. This might include shelving or drawers for materials and a flat surface, like a desk or easel, suited to your preferred medium.

Your art space should be inviting, a place that calls you to come and create. Personalize it with inspirational items such as art books, images of your favorite artworks, or objects from nature that spark your creativity. This environment not only supports your artistic endeavors but also serves as a sanctuary, a personal retreat where you can immerse yourself in the joy of creating, exploring, and expressing through art.

5.2 Crafting Your Story: Creative Writing Workshops

The blank page beckons, a silent yet potent invitation to spill your thoughts, weave narratives, or articulate insights that have been shaped by a lifetime of experiences. As you contemplate where to begin, consider the vast expanse of genres at your disposal, each offering a different avenue for storytelling and personal expression. Whether it's the structured cadences of poetry, the immersive world-building of fiction, or the introspective exploration of memoir writing, every genre holds the potential to mirror a facet of your life or ignite your imagination. Finding your voice—a true reflection of your inner self and unique perspectives—is not about conforming to a predefined style but about discovering how best to express your thoughts and feelings. This journey of discovery is deeply personal and can be profoundly rewarding.

To embark on this explorative process, start by reading widely across genres. Dive into mystery novels, historical fiction, biographies, and more. Notice which styles resonate with you, which narratives draw you in, and what it is about the writing that speaks to you. Is it the rhythmic beauty of a well-crafted poem, the raw honesty of a personal essay, or the suspenseful buildup of a thriller? As you expose yourself to different forms of writing, try your hand at short pieces in various styles. This practice not only hones your skills but also helps clarify what feels most natural and fulfilling to write about. Remember, your voice might blend elements from multiple genres, creating a hybrid that is uniquely yours.

Participating in creative writing workshops can significantly enhance this journey of finding and refining your voice. These workshops provide a structured yet flexible environment where you can experiment with different styles under the guidance of experienced instructors. The immediate feedback from peers and mentors is invaluable, offering new perspectives on your work and constructive criticism that encourages growth. Furthermore, these workshops often foster a sense of community among participants, creating a supportive network of fellow aspiring writers who share the passion for storytelling and personal expression. This community can be a source of inspiration and motivation, pushing you to refine your craft and explore new creative territories.

The road from penning a story to sharing it with the world can be as daunting as it is exciting. Fortunately, today's literary landscape offers numerous avenues for publishing your work. For those looking to start small, local newsletters or community magazines can be ideal platforms. These publications often welcome contributions from local residents, providing an opportunity to share your stories or poems with a familiar audience. As your confidence grows, you might consider broader platforms such as literary journals or online blogs that cater to larger audiences. For those who dream of compiling their stories or poems into a book, self-publishing presents a viable option. Platforms like Amazon's Kindle Direct Publishing allow you to publish your work digitally and reach readers globally without the need for traditional publishing gateways.

Navigating these publishing options can be overwhelming, but numerous online resources and communities are available to help aspiring writers learn from and support each other through these processes. Websites like Writers Digest offer comprehensive guides on everything from writing tips to publishing advice, while online forums such as Absolute Write Water Cooler allow writers to exchange insights and experiences. For more structured learning, platforms like Coursera and Udemy offer courses on creative writing and publishing that are taught by industry professionals. These resources not only provide practical knowledge but also help you connect with a global community of writers, expanding your network and exposing you to new opportunities and perspectives in the world of writing.

5.3 Music as a Retirement Hobby: Learning an Instrument

The melodious journey of learning to play a musical instrument in retirement is not just about mastering the notes but also about enriching your life with joy and cognitive stimulation. The process begins with selecting the right instrument, one that not only aligns with your musical tastes but also fits your physical capabilities and lifestyle. Considerations such as the size of the instrument, the level of physical effort required, and the ease of learning are crucial. For example, a ukulele, with its small size and relatively simple chord structures, can be an excellent choice for those looking for an easy-to-learn string instrument. On the other hand, a keyboard might appeal to those who enjoy a wide range of sounds and the possibility of playing both melody and harmony. For those with joint issues or reduced lung capacity, lighter, less physically demanding instruments like the harmonica or an electronic piano can provide comfort and enjoyment.

Once the choice of instrument is made, the benefits of embarking on this musical adventure become readily apparent. Cognitive benefits, particularly, are a significant aspect of learning music. Engaging in musical activities stimulates various areas of the brain responsible for memory, coordination, and reasoning. Studies have shown that adults who play musical instruments are less likely to develop cognitive impairments as they age. Moreover, the process of learning and playing music can improve your attention to detail, enhance auditory and motor skills, and boost your problem-solving abilities. Beyond the cognitive enhancements, the emotional rewards of playing music are profound. Music can elevate your mood, reduce stress, and provide a sense of accomplishment. It also offers a form of emotional expression that can be therapeutic, allowing you to communicate feelings that might be difficult to articulate through words alone.

Finding suitable music lessons tailored for adult learners is the next step in your musical exploration. Many community centers and music schools offer classes designed for older adults, recognizing that the pace and style of teaching suited to younger people might not be ideal for retirees. These classes often focus more on enjoyment and gradual progress rather than rigorous practice schedules. Additionally, private tutors can provide personalized guidance, adjusting the pace and content of lessons to match your individual learning style and goals. Online music lessons are also an increasingly popular option, offering the convenience of learning from home and the ability to revisit lessons as needed. Websites like YouTube have myriad tutorials that can help beginners take the first steps in learning how to play an instrument. For more structured learning, platforms like MasterClass or Lessonface connect you with experienced musicians who provide live, interactive lessons online.

Patience and regular practice are essential components of learning to play an instrument. Initially, progress might seem slow, and the physical act of playing can be challenging. Regular practice is crucial, as it helps build the muscle memory needed to play the instrument proficiently. Establishing a routine practice schedule that fits into your daily life is beneficial. Even short, daily practice sessions can lead to significant improvements over time, more so than sporadic, longer sessions. It's important to set realistic expectations and celebrate small victories along the way—whether it's mastering a new chord or playing through a whole song without mistakes. Remember, the goal is not only to play music but to enjoy the process of learning and making music, which enriches your life and keeps your mind active and engaged.

As you integrate music into your daily routine, consider sharing your musical journey with others. Playing music with friends, joining a local amateur musical group, or even performing for family can enhance your enjoyment and provide motivation to continue learning. These social interactions can also reinforce the skills you've learned and provide joyful communal experiences through shared musical endeavors, making every note played a step towards a more vibrant and melodious life.

5.4 Photography: Capturing Life's Moments

Photography stands as a profound avenue for personal expression and a dynamic way to engage with the world around you. Beginning your photographic journey involves understanding the fundamental tool of this art form—the camera. Selecting a camera that aligns with your needs depends on what you aim to capture and how deep you wish to dive into the technical aspects of photography. For most beginners, a simple point-and-shoot camera offers ease of use with automatic settings that adjust focus and exposure to suit various lighting conditions. However, if you're inclined towards more control over your images, a digital single-lens reflex (DSLR) camera provides manual options to adjust shutter speed, aperture, and ISO settings, which can be learned gradually as your interest and skills develop.

Familiarizing yourself with the basic settings of your chosen camera is crucial. Spend time reading the manual or watching tutorial videos specific to your model to understand each function. Key settings that significantly affect how your photos turn out include the aperture, which controls the depth of field; the shutter speed, which affects the clarity of moving objects; and ISO, which determines the sensitivity of your camera's sensor to light. Experimenting with these can help you grasp how each setting impacts your photos, guiding you through the process of finding your photographic style. Whether capturing the serene motion of a cityscape at night or the vibrant chaos of a family gathering, each setting allows you to manipulate how you frame and interpret the scene before you.

Photography goes beyond mere technique; it is a powerful form of personal expression. It allows you to capture moments not just as you see them, but as you feel them, turning everyday scenes into profound expressions of life's beauty and complexity. Through your lens, mundane moments can be transformed into powerful narratives or abstract compositions that evoke emotion and thought. The act of choosing what to capture, from a grand landscape to the intricate details of a street corner, reflects your perspective and can convey your feelings and thoughts to others. This expressive power not only enhances your creative skills but also deepens your connection to the environments and communities you photograph, fostering a richer appreciation of the world around you.

Joining photography groups can significantly enrich your journey into photography. These groups offer a blend of inspiration, education, and companionship that is invaluable for both novice and experienced photographers. Local photography clubs often organize regular meetings, workshops, and outings, providing opportunities to learn from more experienced photographers and to practice new skills in a supportive environment. For those who prefer the flexibility of connecting with fellow photography enthusiasts online, numerous forums and social media groups offer a platform to share your work, receive feedback, and participate in challenges that can stretch your creativity and technical skills.

Engaging with these communities not only accelerates your learning curve but also opens up avenues for exhibitions or collaborative projects that can enhance your visibility and experience in the field. These interactions, whether in person or online, can be particularly motivating, pushing you to refine your technique and explore new subjects and styles. The feedback and discussions help you see your work from different perspectives, which is crucial for artistic growth. Additionally, photography groups often provide a sense of belonging and a shared passion that can make your photographic endeavors more enjoyable and rewarding.

Embarking on photo projects can be a fantastic way to focus your photographic practice and develop your skills systematically. Projects can vary widely depending on your interests and goals. For instance, a 365-day project, where you commit to taking one photo every day for a year, can be an excellent way to cultivate discipline and creativity, forcing you to look at your everyday environment through a fresh, artistic lens. Alternatively, thematic projects such as documenting the lives of local artisans, focusing on urban street art, or capturing the changing seasons in a beloved landscape can provide deeper engagement with a particular subject or community.

These projects not only challenge you to develop consistency and patience but also allow you to see gradual improvements in your work. They can culminate in a comprehensive portfolio that showcases your style and skills, possibly leading to exhibitions or publications. Moreover, the focused nature of a project can provide a narrative thread that engages viewers, offering them a window into your unique artistic perspective and the stories you wish to tell through your lens. As you progress, consider sharing your project's development online or through local exhibits, which can offer additional feedback and recognition of your artistic journey.

As you continue to explore the vast possibilities within the realm of photography, each image you capture not only serves as a reflection of the world around you but also as an imprint of your personal growth and creative expression. Embrace each opportunity to press the shutter as a moment to learn, to express, and to connect, continually expanding the horizons of your photographic journey.

5.5 Joining a Book Club: Reading for Pleasure and Discussion

The allure of a good book is timeless, offering a portal to different worlds, perspectives, and experiences. For retirees, joining a book club can enrich this reading experience, transforming it from a solitary activity into a shared exploration of narratives and ideas. The first step in this enriching endeavor is to find a book club that aligns with your interests and reading pace. Consider what genres captivate you—are you drawn to historical fiction, intrigued by mystery novels, or inspired by biographies? Identifying your preferences helps narrow down the search for a club that matches your tastes. Local libraries, bookstores, and community centers often host book clubs and can be excellent starting points. These institutions typically offer a range of genre-specific clubs, which can enhance your chances of finding a group that reads at your desired pace and engages in discussions that interest you.

Another option is to utilize online platforms such as Meetup, where you can search for book clubs in your area or even virtual clubs that meet online. These platforms allow you to browse different groups and see upcoming reading selections and meeting schedules, helping you choose a club that fits seamlessly into your lifestyle. Additionally, many online book clubs are now facilitated via video calls, making participation possible from the comfort of your home. This convenience is particularly beneficial if mobility or transportation is a concern, or if you prefer the flexibility of connecting with readers not just in your locality but across the globe.

Participating in a book club offers numerous benefits that go beyond the joy of reading. Socially, book clubs provide an opportunity to meet new people and form friendships with those who share similar interests. These gatherings are not just about discussing books but also about sharing life experiences and perspectives, which can be especially valuable in retirement. The sense of community and belonging that comes from regular meetings with a book club can significantly enhance your social well-being and keep feelings of loneliness at bay. Cognitively, the act of reading and discussing literature can be a great mental workout. Engaging actively with a book—analyzing characters, uncovering themes, and debating interpretations—stimulates the brain and can improve cognitive functions such as memory, critical thinking, and concentration.

For those who find existing book clubs do not meet their needs or who are looking for a more leadership-oriented role, starting your own book club is a rewarding option. Begin by deciding on the structure and focus of your club. Will you choose books from a specific genre, or will each member have a chance to select a book on a rotating basis? Establishing clear guidelines on how books are chosen and discussions are conducted helps ensure the club runs smoothly. Next, consider the size of the group. A smaller number of participants might allow for deeper discussions where everyone has a chance to speak, while a larger group might offer a wider range of perspectives and insights.

The format of the meetings should also be planned. Decide whether you will meet in person, online, or a hybrid of both. Each format has its benefits and challenges, and your choice may depend on the preferences and circumstances of the group members. Additionally, create a welcoming and respectful atmosphere where all members feel comfortable sharing their views. Encourage discussions that are not just about critiquing the book but also about connecting the themes of the book to personal experiences and broader social issues, which can enrich the conversation and make the meetings more engaging and meaningful.

Online book clubs have gained popularity for their convenience and the diversity of participants they can attract. Platforms like Goodreads offer tools to create and manage book clubs, facilitating discussions through forums or virtual meetings. These clubs can be particularly appealing if you are looking for flexibility in participation or wish to connect with readers who have specific literary interests that might not be as common locally. When managing an online book club, it's important to keep the discussions organized and inclusive. Regular updates, clear communication about reading schedules, and structured discussion threads help maintain engagement and ensure that all members feel involved. Additionally, utilizing video conferencing tools for meetings can add a personal touch, making discussions more dynamic and interactive.

As you delve into the world of book clubs, each book read and discussed not only enriches your understanding of the world but also deepens your connections with fellow readers, creating a tapestry of shared literary journeys that enhance the pleasure of reading.

5.6 DIY Home Projects: From Concept to Creation

Embarking on a DIY home project can be both exhilarating and daunting, especially if you're new to the world of do-it-yourself endeavors. The key to a successful project lies in meticulous planning, which involves more than just sketching out ideas—it requires thoughtful consideration of budget, design, and the sequence of tasks. Firstly, defining the scope of your project is essential. Decide whether you're looking to renovate a room, build a piece of furniture, or perhaps create an outdoor space. Once the scope is defined, drawing up a detailed plan can help visualize the end result. Utilize design software or simple graph paper to layout dimensions and placement, which can prevent potential issues during the build phase.

Budgeting is another critical aspect of planning. It ensures that your project is financially feasible without compromising on quality. Start by listing all the materials you'll need, then research and compare prices from various suppliers. Don't forget to include tools and equipment in your budget. If some tools are too expensive for one-time use, consider rental options which can significantly reduce your outlay. Additionally, set aside a contingency fund, usually 10-20% of the total budget, to cover unexpected expenses. This proactive approach can help keep your project on track financially and reduce stress as you progress.

Building the necessary skills for DIY projects is not as intimidating as it might sound. Many community colleges offer classes in basic carpentry, plumbing, or electrical work, providing hands-on experience and expert guidance. Online tutorials are another invaluable resource. Platforms like YouTube have countless DIY channels where skilled crafters demonstrate processes step-by-step, from basic techniques to more advanced projects. These resources not only enhance your skills but also boost your confidence in handling various tools and materials. Remember, the goal is to build your competency gradually, project by project, ensuring that with each new endeavor, you become more proficient and self-reliant.

Safety is paramount when undertaking any DIY project. Before starting, familiarize yourself with the proper use of each tool and always follow the manufacturer's guidelines. Invest in essential safety gear such as goggles, gloves, and ear protection, and ensure your workspace is well-ventilated, especially if you're working with paints or solvents. Keep a first aid kit readily accessible and make sure you know the basics of treating minor injuries. It's also wise to inform someone else about your project plans, particularly if you're working alone. This attention to safety not only prevents accidents but also ensures that your DIY activities are enjoyable and free from unnecessary risks.

Utilizing community resources can greatly enhance the scope and enjoyment of your DIY projects. Many cities have tool libraries where you can borrow tools for a nominal fee, which is particularly useful for expensive tools that you may not use frequently. Some communities also offer maker spaces or workshops where individuals can access professional-grade tools and equipment. These spaces often foster a collaborative environment where you can share ideas and learn from more experienced DIY enthusiasts. Additionally, local hardware stores sometimes conduct free workshops that can provide you with practical skills and knowledge about the latest materials and technologies. Leveraging these resources not only supports your projects but also connects you with a network of like-minded individuals who can offer support and inspiration.

As you reflect on the transformative potential of DIY projects, consider how each task you undertake not only beautifies your space but also builds your self-reliance and creativity. The skills you develop, the plans you conceptualize, and the safety measures you learn enrich your life beyond the immediate scope of any single project. These endeavors cultivate a sense of accomplishment and pride that resonates through all areas of life, reinforcing the joy and fulfillment that come from creating and problem-solving with your own hands.

Looking ahead, the next chapter will explore the enriching world of outdoor and nature activities, where the skills and confidence you've gained from DIY projects can be applied in new, exciting ways. Whether it's building a garden shed, crafting a birdhouse, or simply appreciating the practical skills you've developed, the upcoming chapter will expand the horizons of your active and engaged lifestyle.

Interactive Element: Awakening your creativity

Which of these activities appeals to your creative nature. Plan your first foray into unleashing your inner artist

- Art
- Writing
- Music
- Photography
- Reading
- DIY

In her thirties, Sue embarked on a new journey, retraining as a Speech and Language therapist and dedicating many years to the UK's National Health Service. By the time she reached her mid-fifties, Sue found herself working part-time. Retirement wasn't initially on her radar, but mounting frustrations at work ignited a longing for a different life. With careful budgeting, she realized she could afford to retire and bravely did so at 57.

During her part-time work, Sue had started volunteering for the National Trust, a conservation charity, at a nearby large garden park. Upon retiring, she expanded her involvement, taking on roles in the bookshop and as a guide for visitors. A passionate cinema enthusiast, she also volunteered as an usher at the local independent cinema, contributing to screenings tailored for people with autism and dementia.

These volunteer roles not only provided Sue with a sense of purpose but also broadened her social horizons, leading to new friendships and a vibrant social circle. Living in Lewes, South England, she indulged in frequent holidays, mainly exploring Britain by train, although rarely for more than a week at a time.

When Sue was 63, her mother's passing prompted a period of introspection. Realizing her health and love for independent travel and mountain climbing might not last forever, she decided to act on her long-standing love for the Lake District, a picturesque national park in northwest England.

This year, in mid-April, Sue embarked on a new adventure. She packed her essentials, left her house, and headed to the Lakes with an open-ended plan. Staying in holiday cottages for flexibility, she funded her journey with her pension and a small inheritance. Sue immersed herself in walking, exploring, and quickly found a new social circle. She resumed her role as a National Trust volunteer, joined a walking group, and became part of a wild swimming group. She participates in a singing group and has tried some new activities like kayaking.

Sue's new chapter is filled with excitement and fulfillment. Living alone, she is far from lonely, having met numerous wonderful new people. She continues to embrace her adventure, savoring every moment of her vibrant, independent life.

6. Outdoor and Nature Activities

Engaging with nature and the outdoors offers a great blend of serenity and stimulation and provides a backdrop for a number of activities that enhance your health and wellbeing. The benefits of being out in nature have been well documented, not just for physical but for mental health too. Imagine stepping outside and the fresh air greeting you like and old friend. From the gentle exercise of gardening to birdwatching inviting you to sharpen your senses and cultivate patience, the following activities can help you rediscover the beauty of your environment.

6.1 Community Gardening: Growing Together

Engaging in community gardening presents a unique opportunity to cultivate more than just plants; it fosters relationships, promotes physical activity, and contributes positively to the environment. These gardens become hubs of social interaction, where individuals of diverse backgrounds come together united by a common interest in gardening. The benefits of participating in such a collective endeavor extend well beyond the harvest of fruits and vegetables. Physically, the act of gardening involves various activities like digging, planting, weeding, and watering, which are excellent forms of low-impact exercise that improve endurance, flexibility, and strength. The tasks performed in a garden encourage the use of motor skills while also promoting endurance and flexibility. Moreover, the exposure to sunlight and fresh air contributes to improved mood and health through the natural absorption of vitamin D, which is essential for bone health and immune function.

Environmentally, community gardens play a vital role in enhancing biodiversity, promoting the growth of a variety of plants and providing habitats for numerous species of insects and birds. These gardens often utilize organic gardening practices, which help maintain healthy soil and reduce pollution by avoiding chemical pesticides and fertilizers. The green spaces created by community gardens not only contribute to better air quality but also help in cooling urban areas, thereby reducing the urban heat island effect. In addition to these ecological benefits, the act of growing food locally significantly reduces the carbon footprint associated with transporting food items from distant locations, contributing to a more sustainable lifestyle.

Finding and joining a community garden can be a rewarding venture. Start by searching for existing gardens in your locality. Many cities and towns have public gardens or allotments where plots are available either for free or for a nominal fee. Local government websites, gardening clubs, and environmental groups can be valuable resources for locating these gardens. If there are no existing community gardens nearby, consider starting one. Engage with your neighbors, local schools, or community centers to gauge interest and gather support. Local authorities may offer grants or land use permissions for community projects such as gardening. When planning a community garden, consider accessibility for all potential members, including those with limited mobility. Raised planting beds and wide paths can make the garden accessible and enjoyable for everyone.

Participation in community gardening is not just about growing plants but also about the communal learning experience it offers. Novice gardeners can learn a great deal from more experienced members, gaining knowledge about planting seasons, pest control, soil health, and sustainable gardening practices. Many community gardens organize regular workshops or invite experts to speak on topics ranging from composting to plant nutrition. These learning opportunities allow members to not only improve their gardening skills but also to implement these practices in their own gardens at home, potentially leading to better garden yields and more sustainable practices community-wide.

One of the most joyous aspects of community gardening is the celebration of the harvest. Organizing harvest celebrations can be a wonderful way to enjoy the fruits of the collective labor, strengthen community bonds, and share the bounty with others. These events can include potluck meals, where dishes are prepared using ingredients from the garden, cooking demonstrations, or even small farmers' markets where surplus produce is sold to the wider community. These celebrations not only provide an opportunity for social gathering and fun but also reinforce the sense of community and shared achievement. They highlight the cycle of growth and renewal that community gardens embody, reminding everyone of the rewards that come from working together towards a common goal. Such events also attract new members and can inspire other communities to start their own gardening projects, spreading the benefits of community gardens even further. As you immerse yourself in the rhythms of planting, tending, and harvesting within a community garden, you contribute to a cycle of growth that nourishes both the body and the community, weaving your own story into the larger tapestry of communal living and sustainability.

6.2 Hiking and Nature Walks for All Fitness Levels

Exploring the serenity and beauty of nature through hiking offers a fantastic way to stay active and engaged with the environment. When considering this activity, it's crucial to select trails that align with your physical fitness level and personal interests. For those new to hiking or looking for less strenuous options, seek out flat or gently rolling trails that don't require significant climbing or descending, which are often found in local parks or nature reserves. Websites like AllTrails or local hiking books can be invaluable resources, providing detailed descriptions, difficulty ratings, and user reviews that help you gauge whether a trail is suitable for your abilities and expectations. For those with a keen interest in specific natural features, such as bird habitats, waterfalls, or geological formations, choosing a trail that highlights these elements can enhance the hiking experience, making each step more rewarding.

Preparation is key to ensuring a safe and enjoyable hiking experience. Before heading out, familiarize yourself with the trail through maps and guidebooks, and check local weather conditions to avoid any unpleasant surprises. Essential items for a day hike include appropriate footwear like hiking boots or sturdy shoes that offer support and traction, a map or GPS device, a sufficient amount of water to stay hydrated, and energy-rich snacks. Depending on the length and remoteness of the trail, additional gear such as a first aid kit, a multi-tool, and a whistle can provide security and self-reliance. Dressing in layers allows for adjusting to changing temperatures throughout the day, and a hat and sunscreen protect against sun exposure. For those venturing into areas where weather conditions can change rapidly, carrying a lightweight rain jacket and extra warm clothing is advisable.

Joining a hiking group can significantly enhance the social aspects of hiking, providing camaraderie and shared motivation that can make stepping into nature more enjoyable and less daunting. Many communities offer hiking clubs that organize regular outings, catering to a range of fitness levels and interests. These groups often have experienced leaders who can offer guidance on hiking techniques and information about the natural environment, enriching the experience. Additionally, hiking with a group enhances safety, as there is strength in numbers, particularly in remote areas or more challenging trails. To find a hiking group, check community bulletin boards, search online for local hiking clubs, or visit outdoor equipment stores that often sponsor group hikes. Participating in these groups not only helps maintain an active lifestyle but also builds lasting friendships with fellow outdoor enthusiasts.

The connection to nature that hiking fosters is profound, offering both physical and mental health benefits. Physically, hiking is a cardiovascular exercise that strengthens the heart, builds muscle tone, and improves endurance, all while being relatively low-impact compared to other forms of exercise. The varied terrain of hiking trails helps improve balance and coordination. Mentally, spending time in nature can reduce stress and anxiety, with the natural environment acting as a calming backdrop that contrasts sharply with urban settings. Studies have shown that regular exposure to nature can lower blood pressure, reduce the symptoms of anxiety and depression, and even boost the immune system. The rhythmic pattern of walking and the sensory experience of being surrounded by nature can also induce a meditative state, helping to clear the mind and restore focus. As you immerse yourself in the sights, sounds, and smells of the trail, you engage in a form of mindfulness that enhances your well-being, making each hike not just a physical journey but a therapeutic retreat into the natural world.

6.3 Bird Watching: Discovering Nature's Melodies

Getting Started

Bird watching, or birding, is a delightful hobby that connects you with nature and offers an escape from the hustle of everyday life. To begin, you'll need a few basic pieces of equipment: a good pair of binoculars, a field guide to help identify different bird species, and a sturdy notebook for logging your sightings. Binoculars with a magnification of 8x42 are recommended for beginners as they offer a stable image and a wide field of view, making it easier to track birds in their natural habitats. A field guide, whether in book form or as an app on your smartphone, is indispensable for learning to recognize various species and understanding their habits and calls. As you venture into your local park or nature reserve, start by tuning into the bird calls and observing the environment. Look for movement in trees and bushes and use your binoculars to get a closer look when you spot a bird.

Joining Bird Watching Groups

While birding can be a solitary activity, joining a local bird watching group can greatly enhance the experience. These groups often organize guided walks, led by experienced birders who can point out species you might overlook and share insights about local bird behaviors and habitats. Participating in these walks not only deepens your knowledge but also connects you with a community of like-minded individuals who share your enthusiasm for nature. This social aspect can be particularly rewarding, transforming bird watching into an opportunity for friendship and learning. To find a group near you, check with local nature centers, wildlife organizations, or birding clubs. Many of these groups welcome people of all skill levels, offering a supportive and educational environment for both novice and experienced birders.

Benefits of Bird Watching

The benefits of bird watching extend far beyond the simple pleasure of seeing beautiful birds. This activity encourages mindfulness and relaxation, drawing your focus away from daily stresses and immersing you in the present moment. The quiet, meditative hours spent waiting for a glimpse of a bird can be profoundly calming, helping to reduce anxiety and improve your overall mental health. Furthermore, the practice of quietly observing and listening sharpens your sensory awareness, enhancing your attention to detail and deepening your appreciation for the subtle complexities of nature. These moments of connection can have a lasting impact, fostering a greater sense of peace and contentment that you carry with you beyond the birding trail.

Documenting Your Discoveries

Keeping a bird watching journal is a wonderful way to document your discoveries and track your progress as a birder. Each entry can include the date, location, weather conditions, and details of the birds you observe, such as species names, behaviors, and personal notes about your experience. Over time, this journal grows into a personal nature diary, reflecting your journey through the world of bird watching. For those inclined towards photography, capturing images of the birds you encounter can add another layer to this hobby. Photographing birds requires patience and skill, and provides a rewarding challenge that combines art with observation. Sharing these photos and notes with your birding group or on online forums can also contribute to citizen science projects, helping to track bird populations and migration patterns, which is crucial for conservation efforts.

In embracing bird watching, you embark on a journey that nourishes your mind, body, and soul. It's an invitation to slow down, observe the often-overlooked beauty of the natural world, and find a harmonious rhythm in the quiet spaces where nature speaks. Whether you're peering through binoculars at a rare bird or jotting down notes in your journal, each moment spent bird watching connects you more deeply to the world around you, enriching your life with every discovery.

6.4 Fishing: Patience, Peace, and Pleasure

Fishing is more than just a pastime; it's an activity that intertwines skill, patience, and an appreciation for the tranquility of nature. For those new to this serene sport, understanding the basics is essential. The fundamental equipment needed includes a fishing rod and reel, a selection of hooks, some weights, floats, and perhaps most importantly, bait. The type of bait used can vary widely depending on the kind of fish you're aiming to catch and may include live bait such as worms or crickets, or artificial baits like spinners and flies. Each piece of equipment plays a pivotal role in the fishing experience and selecting the right gear can significantly enhance your chances of a successful outing. The rod and reel should match the type of fishing you plan to do; lighter gear is typically sufficient for freshwater fishing in lakes and streams, while heavier tackle is needed for saltwater fishing where the fish are generally larger and stronger.

Embarking on this new hobby means choosing between different types of fishing, each offering unique challenges and rewards. Freshwater fishing, the most accessible type, is practiced in rivers, lakes, and streams and is ideal for beginners due to the typically calm waters and the variety of species that can be caught, from trout to bass. Saltwater fishing can be more challenging due to the larger body of water and the size of the fish, but it also offers the excitement of catching larger species such as tuna or marlin. For those interested in a more active fishing style, fly-fishing involves casting artificial flies that mimic real insects on the surface of the water, requiring precise techniques and a great deal of patience. Each type of fishing requires some basic knowledge about where fish are likely to be found during different times of the day or year, and how to attract and catch them, which can be learned through local fishing classes, guides, or experienced fishing buddies.

The practice of ethical fishing is crucial not only for conservation efforts but also for maintaining the natural balance of the ecosystems where fishing occurs. Catch and release is a common practice among sport fishers, which involves careful handling and immediate release of caught fish back into their habitat, ensuring their survival and contributing to the health of the fish population. It's essential to familiarize yourself with local regulations and restrictions, which might dictate the size and number of fish that can be legally caught and kept. These regulations are designed to prevent overfishing and to protect vulnerable species, ensuring that fishing activities do not lead to environmental degradation or the diminishing of fish stocks.

Fishing, with its inherent need for quiet observation and stillness, naturally lends itself to meditation. The rhythmic casting of the line, the focus required to bait a hook, the patience needed to wait for a bite, all contribute to a mindful experience that can be incredibly soothing and mentally rewarding. This meditative quality makes fishing a perfect retreat from the stresses of daily life, offering a moment of calm and a chance to reconnect with nature. The gentle lap of water, the whisper of the breeze, the occasional call of a bird, all these elements combine to create a peaceful atmosphere that can help quiet the mind and foster a deep sense of relaxation. This connection to the natural world revitalizes the spirit, providing a fresh perspective and a renewed appreciation for the simple joys of life.

By engaging in fishing, you not only gain a hobby that enhances your physical and mental well-being but also develop a deeper appreciation for the environment and the importance of preserving our natural resources. Whether you are casting a line from a quiet lakeside or wading through a flowing river, fishing offers a unique blend of challenge, peace, and pleasure, making it a rewarding addition to anyone's leisure activities. As you prepare your tackle box and set out for your next fishing adventure, remember that each outing is an opportunity to learn something new, whether it's mastering a fishing technique, understanding more about aquatic ecosystems, or simply enjoying the tranquility of being at one with nature.

6.5 Camping Adventures for Beginners

Preparing for Your First Camping Trip

For those contemplating their first foray into camping, the thought of sleeping under the stars and waking up to the sounds of nature is alluring yet may seem daunting. To ensure your initial camping experience is enjoyable and stress-free, comprehensive preparation is essential. Start with selecting the right equipment; a quality tent is your first line of defense against the elements, so choose one that is easy to set up and appropriate for the season in which you plan to camp. A sleeping bag rated for the temperatures you expect to encounter is crucial for comfort and safety. Additionally, a sleeping pad or an air mattress not only provides insulation from the cold ground but also significantly enhances sleeping comfort.

Choosing a campsite is equally important. For beginners, established campgrounds with amenities such as running water, restrooms, and fire pits provide a good balance between experiencing nature and having some home comforts. These sites often also offer the security of being close to other campers and park staff, which can be reassuring for those new to outdoor sleeping. Research campsites in advance to understand their facilities and rules, particularly regarding wildlife and fire safety. Reserve your spot if required, as popular locations can fill up quickly, especially during peak travel seasons.

Packing effectively is key to a successful camping trip. Create a checklist to ensure you bring all necessary items including clothing for all weather conditions, cooking supplies, food, water, and a first aid kit. It's advisable to pack layers of clothing to accommodate changing weather; this includes moisture-wicking garments to keep dry and a waterproof jacket in case of rain. Plan your meals in advance, considering easy-to-prepare and nutritious options that will keep you energized for hiking and other activities. Don't forget essentials like a flashlight or headlamp, extra batteries, a multi-tool, and matches or a lighter in a waterproof container. A well-thought-out packing strategy not only prevents leaving behind essential items but also helps in managing the load, making it easier to set up and enjoy your camping experience.

Camping Safety

Once the excitement of setting up camp has passed, maintaining safety becomes the priority. Familiarize yourself with the campground's rules and any potential hazards specific to the area. If you are camping in a region known for its wildlife, educate yourself about the animals you might encounter and how to store food properly to avoid attracting them to your campsite. Most campgrounds provide food lockers, or you might need to use bear-proof containers if camping in bear country. Always keep a clean campsite, and store food and scented items securely.

Understanding how to deal with different weather conditions is crucial. Always check the weather forecast before your trip and prepare for changes. If you find yourself caught in a storm, know the safety protocols such as avoiding open fields, staying low, and avoiding tall isolated trees during thunderstorms. Learn the signs of hypothermia and heat exhaustion, as both can be risks depending on the weather conditions. Ensuring that everyone in your party knows these safety guidelines can prevent accidents and ensure that help can be administered quickly if needed.

Fire safety is another critical aspect. Only use designated fire pits and make sure any fire is completely extinguished before you go to sleep or leave the campsite. Keeping a bucket of water or a shovel nearby can be useful in managing errant sparks or embers. By respecting these guidelines, you contribute to the safety of not only your party but also the surrounding environment and fellow campers.

Camp Cooking

One of the joys of camping is cooking over a campfire or a portable stove. Simple, hearty meals are the best for camping as they can be easily prepared with minimal tools. Consider pre-preparing some meals at home, like marinating meats or chopping vegetables, which can be stored in coolers to ease the cooking process at the campsite. Equipment wise, a portable stove, lightweight pots, and a frying pan along with basic utensils such as a spatula, knives, and a cutting board will suffice for most camp cooking needs.

Experiment with recipes that can be cooked over an open fire, like skewers, grilled vegetables, or simple soups and stews. Remember, cooking times might be longer outdoors, especially if you're using a campfire. Always monitor food for safe temperatures to avoid foodborne illnesses. For breakfast, oatmeal mixed with dried fruits or nuts offers a quick, nutritious start to the day, while items like pancakes and eggs require a bit more equipment and time. For a treat, traditional campfire s'mores or roasted marshmallows can provide a sweet end to a day of outdoor activities.

Exploring Nature

Once settled in, take the opportunity to truly connect with nature through a variety of activities. If the campground has nearby trails, start with an easy nature walk to acclimate to the environment. Use this time to observe the local flora and fauna, and maybe bring along a guidebook to help identify different species. For those interested in more structured learning, many campgrounds offer guided walks or educational talks by park rangers which can enhance your understanding of the ecosystem.

At night, stargazing is a must. Away from city lights, the visibility of stars can be breathtaking. A simple star map or an app can help in identifying constellations and planets. For those interested in wildlife, consider quiet early morning or twilight walks when many animals are most active. Always keep a respectful distance and use binoculars for a closer look.

By engaging in these activities, you not only enhance your camping experience but also develop a deeper appreciation for the natural world. Each step into the wilderness is an opportunity to learn, reflect, and rejuvenate, making camping a truly enriching experience. Whether you're setting up a tent, cooking by a fire, or exploring the great outdoors, each aspect of camping offers a chance to slow down and savor life's simple pleasures, deepening your connection with the natural world and leaving you with memories that last a lifetime.

6.6 Cycling Tours: Exploring Scenic Routes

Embarking on cycling tours offers a refreshing blend of physical activity and scenic exploration that is perfectly suited for retirees looking for leisurely yet engaging outdoor experiences. When selecting the right bicycle for these excursions, comfort and ease of use are paramount. Ideal choices for leisurely tours are hybrid bikes, which combine the lightweight frame of a road bike with the more robust tires of a mountain bike, offering a comfortable ride on various surfaces. For those who prioritize comfort, especially over longer distances, recumbent bikes provide a low-impact ride with a reclined seating position, which is easier on the back and joints. Electric bikes (e-bikes) are another excellent option, as they come equipped with battery-powered "pedal assist" technology, which can be particularly helpful for tackling hills or long distances, allowing you to enjoy the journey without undue strain.

Planning your route is a critical step in ensuring enjoyable and manageable cycling tours. Start by identifying bike-friendly paths that offer safe and scenic routes. Many cities and regions provide dedicated cycling paths that are separated from vehicle traffic, offering a peaceful ride with beautiful vistas. Utilizing online resources such as Google Maps or specific cycling apps like Komoot can help you plot a route that matches your fitness level and interests. These apps often provide detailed information about the terrain, distance, and points of interest along the way, allowing you to tailor your journey to include picturesque spots, cultural landmarks, or pleasant rest areas. For an enriched experience, consider routes that loop through local parks, coastlines, or historical sites, where the natural and cultural environment adds layers of enjoyment to your cycling adventure.

Joining organized group rides or cycling clubs can significantly enhance the social and safety aspects of your cycling tours. These groups often organize regular rides, providing an opportunity to meet other cycling enthusiasts and explore new routes safely under the guidance of experienced cyclists. Group rides can vary from casual outings to more structured tours, and often cater to different levels of ability and interest, ensuring a suitable pace and environment for everyone. Participating in these rides not only fosters a sense of community and mutual support but also enhances safety, as there is safety in numbers, particularly on less traveled roads or in case of mechanical troubles or emergencies.

The health benefits of regular cycling are substantial and particularly valuable for retirees. As a low-impact exercise that provides cardiovascular conditioning, cycling helps in maintaining heart health and increasing stamina. The consistent pedal action helps in building strength and toning muscles, particularly in the lower body, without the harsh impact associated with some other forms of exercise. Regular cycling can also aid in maintaining flexibility and joint mobility, while the aerobic nature of the exercise is beneficial for weight management and metabolic health. Moreover, the psychological benefits are noteworthy; cycling can reduce stress, enhance mood, and provide a sense of freedom and adventure, contributing to overall well-being.

As this chapter closes, reflecting on the enriching experiences that outdoor and nature activities offer reveals a compelling narrative of engagement, health, and community. From the quiet observation required in bird watching to the shared exertion of group cycling tours, each activity invites you to connect with the world around you in meaningful ways. These experiences not only enhance physical health and mental well-being but also foster connections with others, reinforcing the joy and fulfillment that come from being part of a community. As we turn the page to the next chapter, the exploration continues, promising more opportunities to engage, learn, and grow through new activities and adventures.

Interactive Element: Communing with Nature

Which of these is going to be your first step into getting out there in nature. Start you're your favourite.

- Gardening
- Walking and Hiking
- Birdwatching
- Fishing
- Camping
- Cycling

7. Travel and Exploration

For many, the dream is to spend their retirement travelling as they are freed from the constraints of their working life. However, the reality can be different if for example you are on a budget or you have health concerns. Travel in retirement however isn't just about ticking destinations off on a list; it's a profound engagement with the world around you that can enrich your life with experience and new connections. You can do that whether your journey is short of long. Imagine the thrill of watching the horizon from a hot air balloon or feeling the timeless pulse of history while visiting an ancient monument. This chapter is dedicated to transforming your travel dreams into reality, offering a structured approach to planning, preparing, and enjoying your adventures with confidence and curiosity.

7.1 Planning Your Bucket List Travel: A Step-by-Step Guide

Identifying Dream Destinations

Start by envisioning where you want to go. This isn't just about places; it's about experiences and what they represent in your life's tapestry. Perhaps you've always wanted to explore your ancestral roots in Ireland, or maybe you dream of a culinary tour through the vibrant markets of Morocco. There may be places in the next state that you have never visited, or sites within your own area. Begin with a tangible list—write these destinations down, creating a visual representation that can serve as both inspiration and a practical planning tool. Consider creating a "travel dream board" adorned with images and notes about each place. This board can be a daily reminder of your goals and a motivational tool as you plan your trips.

Research and Planning

Thorough research is the cornerstone of successful travel planning. Start by gathering as much information as possible about each destination. This includes the best times to visit based on weather, tourist seasons, and local events that might influence your experience. Utilize a mix of resources—travel guides, websites, and forums like TripAdvisor or Lonely Planet where you can read reviews and tips from other travelers. Understanding cultural norms and key attractions helps in crafting an itinerary that is both exciting and respectful of local customs. Engage with interactive travel planning tools available online; these can help you visualize your trip timeline and manage bookings seamlessly.

Budgeting for the Trip

Financial planning is crucial to enjoy your travels without stress. Begin by outlining a budget for each trip, considering all possible expenditures including flights, accommodation, meals, transportation, and entry fees for attractions. Look for early booking discounts, consider traveling during shoulder seasons when prices are lower, and explore package deals that might offer good value. Tools like budget calculators or apps designed for travel budgeting can be very helpful. Remember, flexibility in your plans can lead to savings; for instance, flying mid-week usually offers cheaper fares compared to weekends. If you are going local, there are often discounts available in tourist information centers or local press which you can take advantage of. Senior discounts too can be taken advantage of.

Health and Safety Precautions

As a retiree, paying special attention to health and safety while traveling is imperative. Ensure that you have comprehensive travel insurance that covers potential medical needs abroad, including evacuation if necessary. Consult with your healthcare provider about vaccinations or preventive medications required for certain destinations. It's also wise to have a plan for managing any existing medical conditions while away from home; this includes carrying sufficient medication and having a copy of your prescriptions in case you need to resupply. Keep a list of emergency contacts and know the location of the nearest embassy or consulate, as well as local emergency services for each country you visit.

~

Interactive Element: Planning Your Travel

Consider using an interactive travel planning map that allows you to plot your destinations, add notes, and customize your routes. This tool not only aids in visualizing your journey but can also be integrated with calendars and budgeting tools to keep your travel plans organized and accessible.

You may prefer the travel board option. A big sheet of paper or board with your list on, followed by the information and the budget. Make that list and start to build up the necessary information.

By following these steps, you're not just preparing for trips; you're crafting experiences that will broaden your horizons and enrich your retirement years. Each destination holds the promise of new sights, sounds, and stories; a collection of moments that will weave into the fabric of your life, creating a tapestry rich with the colors of the world.

~

7.2 Solo Travel in Retirement: Tips and Destinations

Solo travel, especially in retirement, opens up a world of personal freedom and profound self-discovery. This form of travel allows you to indulge your curiosities and preferences without compromise, crafting itineraries that resonate deeply with your personal interests and pace. Imagine wandering through the bustling markets of Istanbul at your leisure, or spending hours in the tranquil gardens of Kyoto, all guided by your instincts and interests. Solo travel not only offers this unmatched freedom but also facilitates a unique kind of introspective journey, where moments of solitude become opportunities for reflection and personal growth.

When selecting destinations for solo travel, safety and welcoming environments are paramount. Cities like Vienna, Auckland, and Copenhagen are renowned for their high safety standards and friendly locals, making them ideal for solo travelers. These cities also offer efficient public transportation systems and a wealth of cultural activities, which can enhance your experience and provide easy navigation. For those who enjoy a blend of history and modern convenience, Kyoto stands out as a destination that pairs cultural richness with the safety and cleanliness Japan is known for. Its serene temples and gardens provide a reflective backdrop perfect for solo explorers. Additionally, countries like New Zealand and Canada are not only known for their breathtaking landscapes but also for their hospitable and open-minded people, making solo adventures less daunting and more enjoyable.

Don't forget your own country. There may be regions or states you have never visited. If you are nervous about solo traveling, then local and domestic travel is a great way to start.

Safety remains a crucial consideration when traveling alone, especially for retirees who may be perceived as vulnerable targets in unfamiliar environments. To safeguard your journey, always keep in touch with family or friends back home, updating them regularly about your whereabouts and plans. This not only ensures someone is always aware of your location but also provides a check-in system that can be vital in emergency situations. When exploring new cities, it's wise to carry a map and a charged cell phone with local emergency numbers saved. Avoid displaying valuables openly and be cautious with personal information. Familiarize yourself with common scams in the destination, which are often highlighted in travel forums and guides, to avoid falling prey to them. Simple precautions, like avoiding dimly lit streets at night and keeping a close watch on your belongings in crowded places, can significantly enhance your safety.

For many, the idea of solo travel can seem daunting, particularly if previous travel experiences were always shared. Building confidence for solo adventures starts with small steps. Begin with day trips to nearby towns or cities, exploring local attractions and gaining comfort with navigating new spaces on your own. These short trips build your travel savvy and self-reliance, preparing you for longer journeys. Engaging in local classes or tours during these trips can also boost your confidence, providing structured activities where you can interact with others while still enjoying the independence of solo travel. As confidence grows, gradually extend the distance and duration of your travels, perhaps venturing to a neighboring country or taking a longer domestic trip. Each successful trip fosters greater confidence, slowly painting a picture of the world as a welcoming place brimming with new friends and experiences just waiting to be discovered.

Traveling alone as a retiree offers a unique opportunity to embrace new cultures and experiences at a pace that suits your personal rhythm. It encourages a depth of interaction with your destinations that can lead to meaningful insights and connections. Whether you're sipping coffee in a quaint Parisian café, watching life unfold around you, or navigating the colorful chaos of a Moroccan souk, solo travel offers a spectrum of enriching experiences that promise not only adventure but also profound personal growth. As you pack your bags and set out, remember that each destination holds not just a checklist of sights to see, but a journey into understanding yourself and the world with greater clarity and wonder.

7.3 Cultural Immersion: More Than Just Sightseeing

Engaging deeply with local cultures transforms your travel experiences from mere sightseeing to enriching encounters that broaden your understanding of the world and its diverse communities. As you step into new lands, consider going beyond the typical tourist paths by delving into the heart of local life. One of the most rewarding ways to do this is by participating in community activities or celebrating local festivals. These events offer a unique insight into the values, traditions, and everyday lives of the people. For instance, joining a traditional tea ceremony in Japan, attending a local wedding ceremony in India or participating in a festival particular to one state can provide an intimate glimpse into the cultural significance of these rituals and the communal spirit that pervades them.

Another authentic way to immerse yourself in a culture is through culinary experiences. Every region's cuisine tells a story of its history, geography, and people. Food Tours are now available in many destinations which you can enjoy whether a solo traveler or not as you join a group for a culinary adventure. Engage in cooking classes where local chefs share not just their recipes but also the history and significance of the dishes. Markets are also cultural hotspots where the vibrancy of local life is palpable. Spend a morning at a market, perhaps accompanied by a guide who can provide context to what you see and taste; this could include learning about indigenous ingredients or understanding regional agricultural practices. These culinary experiences allow you to taste the essence of the culture, literally and metaphorically, making your travel experience profoundly more meaningful.

Language Learning Tips

One of the keys to unlocking deeper cultural engagement is learning the local language, at least at a basic level. Language is the gateway to understanding a culture's nuances, humor, and values. Start with practical phrases and greetings, as these can go a long way in showing respect and openness towards the locals. Tools such as Duolingo or Rosetta Stone offer user-friendly platforms for learning new languages through intuitive, daily exercises that make learning less daunting. Even mastering simple phrases such as "Thank you," "Please," and "Good morning" in the local language can enrich interactions, making them warmer and more personal. Additionally, carrying a small phrasebook or a language translation app can help in situations where more complex communication is necessary.

Consider also the cultural context in which language is used. In some cultures, direct communication is appreciated, while in others, indirect expressions are the norm. Being aware of these subtleties can prevent misunderstandings and foster smoother interactions. Engaging locals in conversation, even if imperfectly, often leads to memorable exchanges and can open doors to experiences and insights that are not accessible through guidebooks or tours. Locals tend to appreciate the effort foreign visitors make to speak their language, and this effort can lead to genuine hospitality and deeper friendships during your travels.

Cultural Etiquette

Understanding and respecting local customs and etiquette is crucial for a harmonious travel experience. Each culture has its own set of social norms and practices, and what may be acceptable in one country can be considered rude or inappropriate in another. Before you travel, take time to research the local customs. For example, in many Middle Eastern countries, it is customary to remove your shoes before entering someone's home, while in Japan, it is polite to bow when greeting someone. In Europe, maintaining a certain level of dress code when visiting churches and other religious sites is a sign of respect.

Being cognizant of these practices shows respect for the local culture and minimizes the risk of unintentional disrespect. Observing and adapting to these customs also enriches your travel experience, allowing you to see the world through a different lens and appreciate the diversity of human expression and interaction. Additionally, in places where bargaining is a norm, such as in many Asian markets, understanding the etiquette around negotiation can make the experience more enjoyable and respectful to the vendors.

Authentic Experiences

To truly embrace a culture, seek out experiences that allow you to live as locals do. Homestays are a wonderful way to achieve this, as they provide an opportunity to stay in a local home, often sharing meals and daily routines with your hosts. This intimate experience offers insights into the everyday life of the community, often leading to friendships and a deep appreciation of the local way of life. In many parts of the world, such as in rural Italy or the highlands of Guatemala, homestays also contribute economically to the host families and communities, making your travel experience both culturally enriching and socially responsible.

Participating in local volunteer opportunities can also provide a meaningful way to connect with the community. Whether it's helping in a community garden in a small town or teaching basic English in a village school, these activities can provide a deeper understanding of the local challenges and achievements. They also offer a chance to give back, ensuring that your travel experiences are not just about taking but also about contributing positively to the places you visit.

7.4 Road Trips and RV Living: The Ultimate Freedom

The allure of the open road, with its endless vistas and the freedom to explore at your own pace, is a timeless call to adventure. Planning a road trip involves a blend of excitement and strategy, ensuring that each mile traveled is as enjoyable as the destinations themselves. The key to a successful road trip lies in meticulous route planning that not only targets scenic beauty and key landmarks but also prioritizes comfort and safety. Begin by defining your main points of interest – these could be national parks, historic sites, or family homes. Utilize reliable mapping tools like Google Maps or dedicated route planners that provide options for scenic routes, which often offer more enjoyable driving experiences than direct highway routes. These tools also help identify critical amenities along the way such as rest stops, gas stations, and restaurants, ensuring you never find yourself too far from necessary conveniences.

When planning your route, consider the driving time between stops. Aim for a balance that allows you to enjoy the scenery and attractions without becoming fatigued. Long hours on the road can be taxing, especially if you're not used to extended periods behind the wheel. Incorporate frequent breaks into your itinerary, planning for at least a 15-minute stop every two hours to stretch and refresh. This not only helps maintain your energy levels but also keeps alertness high, which is crucial for safe driving. Moreover, consider the accommodation options available along your route. Whether you prefer hotels, motels, or camping sites, booking in advance can secure you the best spots and often save you money.

The romance of the road is perhaps best experienced in an RV, where the comforts of home meet the thrill of travel. Engaging in RV living requires understanding the basics of choosing and maintaining your vehicle. Your choice of RV should align with your lifestyle and comfort needs; whether it's a compact Class B camper ideal for couples or a larger Class A motorhome that offers ample space for extended stays. Key considerations include the size of the RV, ease of driving, fuel efficiency, and the layout of living spaces. Familiarize yourself with the operation of essential systems such as the electrical, plumbing, and heating to ensure smooth travels. Before embarking on a long journey, it's prudent to take your RV for a shorter trip close to home. This allows you to identify any issues or missing necessities in a relatively safe and convenient environment.

Staying connected with family and friends while embracing the nomadic lifestyle is vital, not only for sharing your experiences but also for safety and peace of mind. Today's technology offers several solutions for staying in touch. Investing in a good quality mobile hotspot can provide you with a reliable internet connection, essential not just for communication but also for navigation and entertainment. Many RV parks and camping sites offer Wi-Fi, but the reliability can vary greatly. As such, having your own dependable internet can make a significant difference. Additionally, social media platforms and blogs are fantastic ways to share your journey with loved ones and the broader community of road trippers and RV enthusiasts. They not only allow you to document your travels but also to receive tips and recommendations from fellow travelers.

Health considerations are paramount when embarking on an extended road trip or living in an RV. Regular movement and stretching are crucial to prevent the stiffness and discomfort associated with long periods of driving. Keep a basic first aid kit in your RV, stocked with necessary medications, bandages, and supplies to manage minor injuries or ailments. Pay attention to your diet; while it's tempting to indulge in fast food, maintaining a balanced diet helps keep your energy levels stable and supports overall health. Ensure you have access to clean water and plan for meals that are nutritious and simple to prepare. If you have ongoing health concerns, keep a record of nearby hospitals or clinics along your route, and ensure you have ample medical supplies for the duration of your trip.

Embracing the RV lifestyle or setting out on a road trip offers a unique blend of freedom, adventure, and the comforts of home. With thoughtful preparation, the right equipment, and a spirit of flexibility, you can ensure that your time on the road is filled with memorable experiences and new discoveries, all while maintaining comfort and safety. Whether you find joy in the quiet of a secluded campsite or the thrill of exploring new cities, road trips and RV living allow you to craft your adventures on your terms, making every journey uniquely yours.

7.5 Cruising as a Senior: What to Know

Cruising offers a splendid way to see the world, especially for retirees who can enjoy the luxury of time and the ease of having all amenities and activities within reach. Selecting the right cruise can make all the difference in your experience. When choosing a cruise that caters to the senior demographic, consider opting for smaller ships. These vessels often offer a more personalized service, shorter queues, and less crowded spaces, which can significantly enhance your comfort and enjoyment. Smaller ships are also able to dock at smaller ports, allowing access to less touristy, more quaint destinations that larger ships cannot reach. Additionally, look for cruises that offer senior-friendly activities. These might include lectures, workshops, and classes that cater to older adults' interests, such as history, art, or cooking, as well as gentler physical activities like yoga or tai chi.

Health and safety are paramount when cruising, particularly for seniors who may have specific medical needs. Most modern cruise ships are well equipped with medical facilities that can handle a range of health issues, from minor ailments to more serious conditions. However, it's essential to check the specifics of these facilities before booking. Ensure that there is always a qualified doctor on board and inquire about the types of medical equipment available. If you have specific medical needs, discuss them with the cruise line ahead of time to ensure they can accommodate you. It's also wise to consider the locations you will be visiting and any vaccinations that might be recommended; your cruise line can often provide guidance on this. Always have an ample supply of any medications you require, as refilling prescriptions aboard or in foreign ports can be challenging.

To truly make the most of your cruise experience, immerse yourself in all the ship and its destinations have to offer. Participate in onboard activities that pique your interest and take advantage of the entertainment options available. Many cruises offer a range of performances, from live music to theatre and dance, providing enriching evenings after your daytime excursions. Additionally, don't hesitate to sign up for shore excursions that allow you to explore the ports you visit more deeply. These excursions are usually organized with reputable providers and can provide fascinating insights into local culture, history, and nature. If mobility is a concern, many cruise lines offer tailored excursions that consider these needs, ensuring everyone has the opportunity to enjoy their time ashore without stress.

Solo cruisers have a unique set of considerations, but many find cruising an ideal way to travel alone due to the built-in social environment and safety of the ship. To avoid the often costly single supplements, look for deals or cruise lines that offer single cabins or are known to reduce or waive these fees during certain periods. Once aboard, take advantage of the social opportunities cruising naturally presents. Many ships organize meet-ups or dining options for solo travelers which can help you connect with other guests. Don't shy away from joining in on group activities or excursions where you can meet like-minded travelers. The structured setting of a cruise can provide a comfortable environment to form new friendships while exploring the globe.

In essence, cruising as a senior offers a wonderful blend of adventure, convenience, and the opportunity to socialize with peers from around the world. By carefully selecting your cruise and engaging fully with the experience, you can ensure a journey that is as relaxing as it is enriching, filled with breathtaking sights, engaging activities, and memories that will last a lifetime. As you step aboard your chosen cruise, embrace the seamless blend of exploration and relaxation that this mode of travel offers, setting the stage for a truly spectacular escape from the everyday.

7.6 Voluntourism: Combining Travel with Giving Back

Voluntourism, where travel intersects with volunteer work, offers a uniquely fulfilling opportunity to experience new cultures while contributing positively to global communities. When selecting a voluntourism project, it's essential to match your personal skills and interests with the needs of the project. Start by assessing your strengths and areas of knowledge—perhaps you have a background in education, healthcare, or construction. Organizations like Projects Abroad or Global Vision International provide platforms where you can filter opportunities based on skill set and interests, ensuring that your efforts will be impactful and meaningful. Research the organizations thoroughly, checking their reputation through reviews and testimonials, and by contacting past volunteers. This due diligence ensures the project's credibility and that your contributions will be ethically used and truly beneficial to the community.

The benefits of voluntourism are manifold, extending beyond the borders of community impact to deeply enrich your own life. On a personal level, engaging in volunteer work in a new environment can sharpen your adaptability, problem-solving skills, and emotional resilience. The challenges of working in unfamiliar settings foster growth and self-discovery, qualities that continue to serve well beyond the trip. From a community perspective, the right voluntourism efforts can lead to sustainable advancement, whether through education, healthcare, or environmental conservation. Projects that focus on teaching English, for instance, can improve local employment opportunities, while those involved in wildlife conservation efforts contribute to preserving ecosystems for future generations.

Preparing for a voluntourism trip requires careful consideration of both cultural and physical elements. Cultural sensitivity training is crucial; understanding the social norms, values, and customs of the community you will be serving helps prevent cultural missteps and deepens the mutual respect between you and the host community. Organizations often provide pre-departure training sessions or resources to equip volunteers with this knowledge. Physically, ensure that you are in suitable health for the activities you'll be involved in, and consult with a healthcare provider if necessary. Pack appropriately for the work and climate —durable clothing, protective gear, and any necessary medications. Being well-prepared allows you to focus on the purpose of your visit, making your contribution more effective and your experience more enjoyable.

Ethical considerations are at the heart of voluntourism. It's vital to engage in projects that have transparent goals and proven benefits to the local community. Avoid those that seem to exploit the vulnerabilities of the community for the sake of tourism. Be wary of projects involving vulnerable populations, like children in orphanages, where short-term involvement may cause more harm than good. Responsible voluntourism should aim to support and empower the community without creating dependency. Opt for projects that work with local leaders and organizations to ensure that the initiatives align with the actual needs of the community and that the effects are sustainable long after you have returned home.

In wrapping up this exploration of voluntourism, remember that combining travel with giving back is not just about the help you provide but also about the connections you build and the global perspective you gain. This approach to travel can transform the way you see the world, making it a deeply enriching part of your life's second chapter. As you close this section, take with you the understanding that travel can be a powerful platform for change, both in the world and within yourself. Looking ahead, the next chapter will build on this theme of transformative experiences, guiding you through managing your retirement finances to support your newfound travel and volunteer endeavors. This financial planning will ensure that your adventures not only fulfill your wanderlust but also sustain your lifestyle and values in the years to come.

Tony and Elizabeth had been married for over 20 years and were in their early fifties when they decided they wanted to live their lives on their own terms. While they don't use the word retired, both of them left the careers they had been working in, Tony as a graphic designer and Elizabeth as an office manager. They decided that with no children they didn't have to worry about leaving an inheritance and would be happy to just earn what they needed to get by. Elizabeth wanted to keep on working part time as she enjoyed the social aspect of working. Tony just wanted to experience new things and have an adventure. One thing he wanted to do was to try living abroad. They bought a small plot of land in a charming village in the Dordogne for a small sum. Tony had plenty of DIY experience and wanted to build his own house.

During the winter months, they worked seasonally in the UK, carefully managing their expenses and saving. Each summer, they would gather the materials they could afford and head to France, in their van. For five leisurely months each year, they camped on their land, working on their house and enjoying bike rides, river swims, and French cuisine.

After ten years of dedication, their house was finally complete. With their seasonal work behind them, they settled back into their hometown during the winters. Elizabeth began volunteering at a local charity shop and got a zero hours contract at a local café – both suited her well as she enjoyed them and they gave the flexibility she needed if they wanted to travel. Tony rekindled his passion for design. Being a tall man, he had always struggled to find shirts that fit well. After taking an evening course in dressmaking with Elizabeth, he started making custom shirts for others with similar issues. What began as a personal project blossomed into a small business, Oblong, fueled by word-of-mouth recommendations. He has plans now to take on an apprentice and pass on his knowledge.

Recently, Tony and Elizabeth sold their house in France to pursue new adventures. They've just set off on their latest journey: cycling around

Holland. With their love for exploration and new experiences, they continue to enjoy their retirement to the fullest.

8. Managing Your Retirement Fun Budget

Imagine a leisurely afternoon, perhaps on a sun-soaked patio with a view of the sea or in a cozy nook of your local library, where the only pressing task is deciding which novel to read or which café to stroll to for dinner. Retirement offers the luxury of unhurried days, but without thoughtful budgeting, even the most carefully planned savings can feel the pinch. In this chapter, you'll discover how to craft a budget that balances your dreams of leisure and adventure with the practicalities of a fixed income, ensuring every little bit you spend enhances your joy and well-being.

8.1 Budgeting for Activities: Maximizing Fun, Minimizing Expense

Creating a Leisure Budget

As with any budgeting, you start with a list of your incomings and outgoings and an assessment of how much you have to dedicate to leisure activities each month. Incomings could include pensions, investments and any part time work. Your outgoings will include housing, utilities, health care and groceries. From the amount you have remaining, you should assign some to cover annual costs like car expenses and insurance. The remainder is your discretionary fund, from which you can carve out a portion specifically for leisure.

It's helpful to categorize leisure spending into tiers based on frequency and cost. For instance, everyday pleasures like reading a book, gardening, or practicing yoga might fall into the first tier with minimal expenses. Occasional indulgences like dining out or theater tickets might form the second tier. Rare splurges, perhaps a cruise or an overseas trip, make up the third tier. Allocating funds across these tiers can help you balance daily enjoyment with saving for big adventures. Tools like financial software or simple spreadsheets can be invaluable here, allowing you to visualize and adjust your budget as your needs and desires evolve.

Prioritizing Activities

Consider what brings you the most happiness. Is it the daily espresso from your favorite café, weekends spent at art galleries, or saving for a dream vacation to Italy? Prioritizing these activities isn't just about cutting costs but about enhancing your life's quality. Reflect on the past month's expenditures, noting which activities were most fulfilling. You might discover that some of the costliest activities brought no more joy than more modest ones. This insight allows you to make informed decisions about where to allocate your funds, ensuring that your spending aligns with your personal values and pleasures.

Cost-Saving Tips

There are numerous ways to enjoy what you love without overspending. For travel, consider going out of season for better rates. Local theaters often offer discounted tickets on less busy nights, and many museums have free entry days. For hobbies like golf or tennis, off-peak memberships can significantly reduce costs. Additionally, embracing community events can offer both social and financial rewards—local concerts, lectures, and classes often come with minimal fees and provide opportunities to meet like-minded individuals.

Tracking Spending

Maintaining a ledger or using a budget tracking app can help you keep a close eye on your leisure spending. Regular reviews will show you where your money goes, highlight any patterns in overspending, and help adjust your budget before small variances turn into large deficits. This habit not only keeps your finances in check but also reassures you that you are living within your means, reducing financial stress and allowing you to enjoy your chosen activities fully.

Interactive Element: Budgeting

Decide on how you are going to manage your budget. You can use a cashbook, a spreadsheet or you may want to consider integrating an interactive budget tracker into your financial planning. This tool can illustrate how adjustments in one area of your budget affect others. For example, reallocating funds from dining out to fund a painting class you've been eyeing. It's a practical resource that supports active management of your leisure budget, ensuring it reflects your current priorities and passions.

- Input your income.
- Input your outgoings.
- Input the monthly proportion of your annual costs.
- How much do you have for Tier 1 activities?
- How much for Tier 2 activities?
- How much for Tier 3 activities?

8.2 Finding Free and Low-Cost Entertainment Options

In your golden years, entertainment doesn't have to be synonymous with extravagant spending. There are myriad avenues through which you can engage in enjoyable activities that require minimal to no financial outlay. Community resources, for instance, are treasure troves of opportunities that await your exploration. Local libraries, beyond lending books, often host free workshops, lectures, and book clubs that can enrich your understanding and skills in a variety of areas. These events not only offer free knowledge and entertainment but also provide a social setting to meet and interact with peers who share similar interests. Similarly, community centers are hubs of activity designed to cater to the community's needs, offering everything from art classes to fitness sessions, many of which are either free or ask for a nominal fee. Exploring these resources can significantly enhance your lifestyle without burdening your wallet.

Local parks are another excellent resource, offering more than just walking trails or picnic spots. Many parks conduct free guided nature walks, bird-watching tours, and even educational talks about local wildlife and plants. These activities allow you to immerse yourself in nature while learning something new each time. The physical activity involved, whether it's a gentle stroll or a more rigorous hike, contributes positively to your health, proving that entertainment can be both enriching and beneficial. Engaging with these community offerings not only helps in keeping your days filled with interesting activities but also plays a crucial role in keeping you physically active and mentally sharp.

Turning to the digital world, the internet is replete with platforms offering free or low-cost courses, workshops, and entertainment suited perfectly for retirees. Websites like Coursera and Khan Academy provide free access to courses on topics ranging from photography to psychology. Similarly, YouTube hosts an array of channels dedicated to teaching everything from cooking and painting to digital skills, all at no cost. For those interested in staying fit, many websites and apps offer free exercise programs that can be done at home, catering to various fitness levels and capabilities. These online resources not only provide flexible learning and entertainment options but also allow you to explore new hobbies and interests from the comfort of your home, making them ideal for days when you prefer staying in.

Volunteering presents a unique blend of giving and receiving that can enrich your life immensely. By donating your time and skills to causes you care about, you not only contribute to the community but often gain free access to events, activities, and experiences. Many cultural festivals, theater productions, and public exhibitions offer free entry to volunteers, providing a wonderful opportunity to enjoy the events you help bring to life. Moreover, volunteering introduces you to a network of like-minded individuals, expanding your social circle and enriching your life with new friendships and interactions. This exchange of time for experience not only fills your days with meaningful activities but also instills a sense of accomplishment and connectivity.

For those who enjoy creative pursuits, there's a vast array of activities that can be both entertaining and cost-effective. Consider nature hikes, which not only provide a great source of exercise but also offer endless opportunities for photography or bird watching, enriching your connection with the natural world. DIY projects can transform home maintenance into an enjoyable pastime, whether you're repainting furniture or creating garden decorations. These projects not only enhance your living space but also provide a profound sense of satisfaction in seeing your efforts materialize. Home-based hobbies such as writing, painting, or crafting can be pursued with minimal investment in materials and can provide hours of peaceful entertainment. Engaging creatively in such activities enriches your daily life, turning routine days into opportunities for expression and innovation.

By exploring these diverse options, you open doors to a world where entertainment and enrichment are readily accessible without straining your finances. Each opportunity not only adds vibrancy to your retirement days but also helps in building a lifestyle that is both rich in experiences and manageable within a budget. As you continue to navigate through your retirement, these resources stand as reminders that life can be abundant and full of wonder, even when you're watching your spending.

8.3 Leveraging Senior Discounts for Leisure and Learning

Exploring the myriad of discounts available to seniors can significantly stretch your retirement budget, allowing you to enjoy a richer, more active lifestyle without compromising your financial health. Many businesses, from travel agencies to local arts centers, offer substantial discounts to seniors, acknowledging the value and contribution of the older demographic. The key to taking full advantage of these discounts is knowing where to find them and how to effectively use them. Start by consulting resources specifically tailored to senior savings. Many websites and organizations curate comprehensive lists of discounts available for everything from airline tickets and hotel bookings to dining and shopping. These resources are invaluable in planning both everyday activities and bigger adventures.

When it comes to travel, many airlines, train companies, and car rental services offer attractive discounts to senior travelers. These discounts can sometimes be as much as 50% off the standard adult rates. However, they might not always be advertised openly. It's advisable to inquire directly with service providers when booking. Similarly, for educational pursuits, numerous online and community-based educational institutions provide reduced or even free tuition rates for seniors. Local community colleges, for example, often have programs allowing seniors to audit classes at no cost, providing a wonderful opportunity to explore new subjects and skills without financial strain.

There are some senior organizations (like AARP in the United States) where membership provides access to an exhaustive array of exclusive deals and perks. In the United Kingdom, the site Restless can point you in the right direction. These organizations negotiate discounts on behalf of their members, covering a wide range of services including health care, travel, and entertainment. The annual fee for such memberships is typically modest compared to the savings they unlock. Beyond tangible savings, these memberships often come with additional benefits such as access to specialized financial advice, health and wellness programs, and invitation to members-only events, all designed to enhance the quality of life in your retirement years.

The practice of simply asking for a senior discount can also yield surprising benefits. Many smaller businesses, including restaurants, theaters, and service providers, offer senior discounts that they don't explicitly advertise. Making it a habit to inquire about such discounts at the point of sale can lead to unexpected savings. This approach requires a degree of assertiveness and a willingness to engage, but the financial rewards can be significant. It is also worth noting that the age at which these discounts apply can vary, with some starting as early as age 50. Therefore, even if you are newly retired, it is worthwhile to start exploring these savings.

Turning to digital resources, several apps and websites are dedicated to helping seniors find discounts. Apps like Sciddy and Senior Discounts Club offer user-friendly interfaces that allow you to search for discounts in various categories based on your location. These platforms are regularly updated, ensuring you have access to the latest information. Moreover, they can be personalized to highlight the types of discounts that most interest you, whether that's dining, entertainment, travel, or shopping. Utilizing these digital tools not only simplifies the process of finding discounts but also helps integrate the habit of discount shopping into your daily routine, making it easier to maintain your financial health while enjoying a vibrant lifestyle.

By embracing these strategies, you empower yourself to make the most of your retirement funds. Leveraging senior discounts effectively means more than just saving money—it's about enriching your life with experiences and opportunities that might otherwise be out of reach. With each discount utilized, you open a door to new adventures, learning experiences, and connections, all while safeguarding your financial future. This proactive approach to budget management ensures that your retirement is not just sustainable, but also vibrant and fulfilling.

8.4 Part-Time Work and Hobbies That Pay Off

Turning your passions into profitable ventures is not only a satisfying way to engage in your hobbies but also a practical approach to supplement your retirement income. Many retirees find that their lifelong hobbies, such as woodworking, knitting, or photography, can generate a meaningful income when positioned correctly in the market. For instance, platforms like Etsy and eBay provide an excellent online marketplace where handmade goods can be sold to a global audience. Similarly, websites like Shutterstock allow photographers to sell their photos. The key is to professionalize your hobby by investing in branding, such as creating an appealing logo and maintaining a consistent quality of products. Marketing your products through social media platforms like Instagram or Pinterest can also significantly enhance your visibility and sales. Additionally, offering personalized classes or workshops in your area of expertise can be a lucrative way to share your skills. Whether it's cooking classes, painting workshops, or music lessons, people appreciate learning from experienced individuals, making this a rewarding way to earn while engaging with your community.

Finding part-time work that aligns with your retirement lifestyle and goals requires a strategic approach. Start by identifying roles that not only cater to your skills and passions but also offer the flexibility to enjoy your retirement. For example, consulting work can often be done remotely and on a project basis, which might provide the perfect balance between working and leisure. Local community centers, libraries, and schools frequently look for part-time instructors or administrative help, offering roles that might not demand long hours but provide meaningful engagement and extra income. Job platforms specifically tailored to older adults, like Seniors4Hire and Retired Brains, can offer targeted job opportunities that match your skill set with employers who value experience and reliability. When exploring these opportunities, it's crucial to clearly communicate your availability and the flexibility you require, ensuring the role enhances your life rather than becoming a burden.

Balancing part-time work with leisure time is essential to ensuring that your employment enhances your retirement rather than detracting from it. Start by setting clear boundaries around your working hours, ensuring they don't interfere with the personal activities and downtime that are important to you. Time management tools, such as digital calendars or planners, can help you visually balance your work commitments with leisure activities, ensuring a harmonious blend that supports a fulfilling retirement lifestyle. It's also helpful to periodically review your work commitments and assess whether they still align with your personal goals. If a job or project becomes too demanding or ceases to be enjoyable, it may be time to reconsider your involvement. Remember, the goal of part-time work during retirement is to complement your lifestyle, not complicate it.

Navigating the tax implications of earning additional income in retirement is crucial to avoid any unwelcome surprises during tax season. Income from part-time work or from selling goods and services is generally taxable, and how this affects your overall tax burden will depend on your total annual income and the tax laws of your state or country. It may be beneficial to consult with a tax professional who can provide guidance specific to your financial situation. They can offer advice on tracking your earnings and deductions, making quarterly tax payments if necessary, and taking advantage of any relevant tax allowances or credits. Keeping meticulous records of all your income and expenses related to your part-time work or hobby business is essential, as this will not only ease the process of filing taxes but can also help in identifying financial trends and areas for improvement in your business.

By transforming hobbies into income streams and finding fulfilling part-time work, retirees can enhance their financial flexibility and personal fulfillment. These activities provide opportunities not only for additional income but also for social engagement, mental stimulation, and personal growth. As you explore these opportunities, remember to maintain a balance that respects your time and aligns with your retirement goals, ensuring that each day is not only productive but also enjoyable and rich with experiences.

8.5 Sharing Economy: Saving Through Swapping and Borrowing

In an era where sustainability and community are becoming increasingly essential, the sharing economy offers a refreshing paradigm of resource utilization that benefits retirees significantly. This socio-economic system involves swapping, sharing, and borrowing goods and services, directly between individuals without the necessity of ownership. This approach not only helps in saving money but also fosters community connections and supports a sustainable lifestyle. For retirees, the sharing economy can provide access to a variety of resources without the burden of full ownership costs or maintenance responsibilities.

Platforms dedicated to fostering these exchanges have flourished, covering a broad range of needs and interests. For instance, websites like Freecycle and Gumtree as well as Buy Nothing groups on social media platforms allow people to give away items they no longer need, and in turn, pick up something useful without any exchange of money. These platforms are particularly beneficial for acquiring or passing on seasonal or rarely used items like gardening tools or holiday decorations, which might not be wise investments at retail price. Similarly, platforms like Tool Library or Library of Things provide community-based sharing services where tools and equipment can be borrowed for a short period. This system is incredibly cost-effective for retirees who may need specific tools for occasional home projects or hobbies.

The concept of bartering, while ancient, has found renewed relevance in the sharing economy. This traditional system involves exchanging goods or services without the use of money. Retirees can leverage their accrued skills and experiences by offering them in exchange for other services. For example, tutoring, gardening, or culinary skills can be traded for services like home repairs, pet sitting, or professional advice. Local barter networks can often be found online, or through community centers, providing a structured environment for these exchanges. Engaging in such barter transactions not only conserves financial resources but also enhances social interactions and community bonding, creating mutual benefits that extend beyond the immediate economic savings.

Community sharing events are another vibrant aspect of the sharing economy that retirees can actively participate in. These events are organized gatherings where community members share and exchange goods and services. Examples include book swaps, seed and plant exchanges, and tool-sharing fairs. Participating in these events can significantly reduce expenses associated with buying new, while also providing a platform to meet neighbors and engage with the local community. These events often create a sense of belonging and collective resourcefulness, which can be especially valuable in fostering social connections in retirement. Organizing such an event can also be a fulfilling project that brings people together and promotes the values of sustainability and cooperation.

By integrating oneself into the sharing economy, retirees not only optimize their expenditures but also participate in a movement that values community engagement and environmental consciousness. This approach to consumption and interaction can significantly enrich a retiree's life, offering practical benefits while also aligning with broader social and ethical goals. Engaging in the sharing economy is not just about saving money—it's about redefining what it means to live resourcefully and communally in a modern world.

8.6 Financial Planning for Bucket List Adventures

When envisioning your retirement, you likely picture yourself finally ticking off those big-ticket items on your bucket list. Whether it's a safari adventure through the Serengeti, a cruise around the world, or a culinary tour through Italy, these dreams require careful financial planning to turn them into reality without jeopardizing your financial security. The first step in this planning process is to set realistic financial goals. Start by listing your dream adventures and researching the approximate costs for each. This research should include all potential expenses—travel, accommodation, activities, and some contingency funds for unexpected costs. Once you have a ballpark figure, it's time to set a savings goal that aligns with your retirement budget and timeline.

Setting a savings timeline is crucial and should realistically reflect your income streams and living expenses. For example, if a dream trip costs $10,000 and you aim to undertake it in five years, you need to save approximately $2,000 a year, or around $167 per month. Automating this savings into a separate travel fund can simplify the process and help prevent these funds from being absorbed into daily expenses. High-yield savings accounts or short-term investments can also help your travel fund grow more quickly, as they offer better returns than regular savings accounts, albeit with slightly higher risks.

Speaking of risks, minimizing financial risk is paramount when planning and booking significant travels. This includes choosing the right time to book to take advantage of lower prices or special promotions. It also involves understanding cancellation policies and considering travel insurance that covers major expenses in case of unexpected events like health issues or family emergencies. Furthermore, diversifying your payment methods can also protect you from potential fraud or disputes; for example, using credit cards for bookings can offer additional protections and benefits like travel insurance or reward points, which can be used to offset other travel costs.

If you are thinking of making a significant investment or even a withdrawal from your retirement fund then consulting with a financial advisor is advisable. An advisor can provide a comprehensive overview of how such spending could impact your long-term financial health. They can offer guidance on how to structure withdrawals to minimize tax implications or suggest investment strategies to fund your travels sustainably. Their expertise can be invaluable in ensuring that your bucket list adventures enhance your retirement rather than compromise it.

By approaching your bucket list with careful planning, clear goals, and informed strategies for saving and spending, you can ensure that these dreams enrich your retirement experience without undermining your financial stability. This proactive and calculated approach to financial planning allows you to embrace your retirement adventures with excitement and peace of mind, knowing that you are on solid financial ground.

As we wrap up this chapter on managing your retirement fun budget, it's clear that a blend of strategic planning, savvy saving tips, and smart spending is crucial for maintaining a balanced and joyful retirement. From leveraging discounts and embracing the sharing economy to setting financial goals for your bucket list adventures, each strategy plays a role in enhancing your lifestyle while protecting your financial future. As we move forward, the next chapter will explore ways to maintain your health and vitality in retirement, ensuring that you can enjoy every moment of your well-planned adventures to the fullest. This natural progression from financial planning to health maintenance underscores the holistic approach needed to ensure a fulfilling and sustainable retirement.

Conclusion

As you come to the end of the book on the journey through this book, it's essential to reflect on the transformation from a structured work-life to a retirement that brims with purpose, health, joy, and ceaseless opportunities for learning and growth. This book has been designed as a beacon to guide you through the often-uncharted waters of post-career life, helping you to anchor your days with activities that not only fill your time but enrich your whole being.

Conclusion

Throughout these pages, we emphasized the paramount importance of embracing new experiences. From diving into health and fitness regimes tailored to various mobility levels, engaging in creative pursuits like painting or writing, to exploring the great outdoors and the digital world, each activity has been chosen to add layers of fulfillment to your life. The diversity of these activities ensures that every day is not just lived but savored, full of new learning and discoveries.

We revisited the adaptability of these activities, ensuring that regardless of your physical condition or financial situation, there is a wealth of options accessible to you. This inclusivity is fundamental, as it underscores the idea that retirement should be liberating, not limiting. The book's unique approach—providing comprehensive guidance on identifying fulfilling activities, effectively managing your retirement budget, and leveraging technology—serves as your toolkit for crafting a personalized, vibrant retirement lifestyle.

A significant portion of our discussion focused on the importance of staying connected. Building new relationships and engaging in community activities are not just social obligations but vital threads in the fabric of a joyful and expansive retirement. The encouragement towards lifelong learning, whether through formal education or casual exploration, supports a mindset that is as youthful and eager as ever.

Now, as you stand at this juncture, ready to step into the retirement you've envisioned, I urge you to take that first step with confidence. Use this book as your roadmap; experiment with different activities, find your tribe, and embrace the myriad opportunities that retirement offers for personal growth and happiness. Remember, the journey to a fulfilling retirement begins with exploring your interests and passions.

I advocate for a retirement filled with continuous exploration and openness to change. As you grow and evolve, so too might your interests and what brings you joy. Stay adaptable, be open to new experiences, and adjust your plans as you learn more about what truly satisfies you.

I invite you to share your retirement journey and successes, no matter how small, with friends, family, or on social media. Each shared story is a stitch in the communal quilt of retired life, offering inspiration and encouragement to others.

On a personal note, as I look towards my own retirement, I am filled with hope and excitement for what lies ahead. I envision days rich with creativity and learning, and I am eager to explore new hobbies and deepen my understanding of the world. Like many of you, I see retirement not as an end but as an inviting new chapter, ripe with potential and unexplored paths.

Thank you for allowing me to be a part of your journey. Here's to a retirement that exceeds your dreams, full of discovery, joy, and the satisfaction of living life to its fullest. Let's step forward together into this new beginning, embracing each day with enthusiasm and anticipation for all the wonderful possibilities it may hold.

If you would like to know more about the author, scan the QR code

References

- *Creating a Retirement Vision Board* https://positivelystacey.com/2018/04/creating-a-retirement-vision-board/
- *Hobbies Seem to Have Universal Mental Health Benefits ...* https://www.forbes.com/sites/andreaanderson/2023/09/14/hobbies-seem-to-have-universal-mental-health-benefits-for-the-elderly/
- *5 Steps to Finding Your Passions After Retirement* https://secondwindmovement.com/finding-passions/
- *11 Meaningful Ways Older Adults Can Volunteer Right Now* https://www.forbes.com/health/healthy-aging/volunteer-opportunities-for-older-adults/
- *Participating in Activities You Enjoy As You Age* https://www.nia.nih.gov/health/healthy-aging/participating-activities-you-enjoy-you-age
- *The Senior's Guide to Online Safety* https://connectsafely.org/seniors-guide-to-online-safety/
- *35 Retirement Party Ideas for Spouse, Parents, Boss* https://parade.com/living/retirement-party-ideas
- *14 Best Senior-friendly Travel Groups* https://www.travelandleisure.com/trip-ideas/senior-travel/best-travel-groups-for-seniors
- *Best tablets for older people to buy in 2024* https://www.radiotimes.com/technology/technology-guides/best-tablets-for-older-people/
- *The Senior's Guide to Online Safety* https://connectsafely.org/seniors-guide-to-online-safety/
- *20 Online Platforms to Learn Anything: Your Ultimate ...* https://launchworkplaces.com/online-learning-platforms/
- *How (and Why) to Blog Your Retirement* https://www.newretirement.com/retirement/blog-your-retirement/
- *Yoga for Healthy Aging: Science or Hype? - PMC* https://www.ncbi.nlm.nih.gov/pmc/articles/PMC8341166/
- *Starting a Walking Club for Older Adults* https://agesafeamerica.com/starting-a-walking-club-for-older-adults/
- *Water Aerobics for Seniors: 12 Pool Exercises You Can Do* https://www.onemedical.com/blog/exercise-fitness/water-aerobics-for-seniors/
- *Brain Training Games Enhance Cognitive Function in ...* https://www.ncbi.nlm.nih.gov/pmc/articles/PMC5930973/

References

- *Participating in the arts creates paths to healthy aging* https://www.nia.nih.gov/news/participating-arts-creates-paths-healthy-aging
- *Starting Out Late: Tips for Senior Writers* https://www.writersandartists.co.uk/advice/starting-out-late-tips-senior-writers
- *Playing an instrument linked to better brain health in older ...* https://medicalxpress.com/news/2024-01-playing-instrument-linked-brain-health.html
- *Crafts for Seniors: 52 Fun and Simple Ideas That Inspire* https://www.greatseniorliving.com/articles/crafts-for-seniors
- *Birdwatching Has Big Mental Health Benefits. How to Start* https://time.com/6231886/birdwatching-mental-health/
- *How to Start a Community Garden | UMN CCAPS* https://ccaps.umn.edu/story/7-effective-steps-start-community-garden
- *Fishing for Beginners | Missouri Department of Conservation* https://mdc.mo.gov/magazines/conservationist/2014-06/fishing-beginners
- *10 Best Easy Trails in Washington* https://www.alltrails.com/us/washington/easy
- *The Cheapest Places to Retire Abroad on $1K Per Month* https://money.usnews.com/money/retirement/baby-boomers/articles/the-cheapest-places-to-retire-abroad-on-1-000-per-month
- *Older Adults and Healthy Travel - CDC* https://wwwnc.cdc.gov/travel/page/senior-citizens
- *The best RVs for full-time living - Roamly* https://www.roamly.com/learning-center/best-rvs-for-full-time-living
- *The Best Volunteer Programs Abroad For Older Adults in ...* https://www.gooverseas.com/blog/best-volunteer-programs-for-older-travelers
- *How to Create a Retirement Budget* https://money.usnews.com/money/retirement/baby-boomers/articles/how-to-create-a-retirement-budget
- *Online Learning for Seniors: 6 Of The Best Free ...* https://www.storypoint.com/resources/health-wellness/online-learning-for-seniors/
- *2024 Best Travel Discounts For Seniors* https://www.theseniorlist.com/senior-discounts/travel/

Printed in Great Britain
by Amazon